MARIJUANA

OPPOSING VIEWPOINTS®

Other Books of Related Interest

MARIJUANA

OPPOSING VIEWPOINTS®

Jamuna Carroll, *Book Editor*

Bruce Glassman, *Vice President*
Bonnie Szumski, *Publisher*
Helen Cothran, *Managing Editor*

OPPOSING
VIEWPOINTS®
SERIES

GREENHAVEN PRESS
An imprint of Thomson Gale, a part of The Thomson Corporation

Detroit • New York • San Francisco • San Diego • New Haven, Conn.
Waterville, Maine • London • Munich

© 2006 Thomson Gale, a part of The Thomson Corporation.

Thomson and Star Logo are trademarks and Gale and Greenhaven Press are registered trademarks used herein under license.

For more information, contact
Greenhaven Press
27500 Drake Rd.
Farmington Hills, MI 48331-3535
Or you can visit our Internet site at http://www.gale.com

Cover credit: © Stockbyte

LIBRARY OF CONGRESS CATALOGING-IN-PUBLICATION DATA

Marijuana / Jamuna Carroll, book editor.
   p. cm. — (Opposing viewpoints series)
Includes bibliographical references and index.
ISBN 0-7377-3323-3 (lib. bdg. : alk. paper) —
ISBN 0-7377-3324-1 (pbk. : alk. paper)
   1. Marijuana. 2. Marijuana abuse. 3. Marijuana—Government policy—United States I. Carroll, Jamuna. II. Opposing viewpoints series (Unnumbered)
HV5822.M3M266 2006
362.29'5—dc22   2005040421

Printed in the United States of America

> "Congress shall make no law... abridging the freedom of speech, or of the press."

First Amendment to the U.S. Constitution

The basic foundation of our democracy is the First Amendment guarantee of freedom of expression. The Opposing Viewpoints Series is dedicated to the concept of this basic freedom and the idea that it is more important to practice it than to enshrine it.

Contents

Why Consider Opposing Viewpoints?

"The only way in which a human being can make some approach to knowing the whole of a subject is by hearing what can be said about it by persons of every variety of opinion and studying all modes in which it can be looked at by every character of mind. No wise man ever acquired his wisdom in any mode but this."

John Stuart Mill

In our media-intensive culture it is not difficult to find differing opinions. Thousands of newspapers and magazines and dozens of radio and television talk shows resound with differing points of view. The difficulty lies in deciding which opinion to agree with and which "experts" seem the most credible. The more inundated we become with differing opinions and claims, the more essential it is to hone critical reading and thinking skills to evaluate these ideas. Opposing Viewpoints books address this problem directly by presenting stimulating debates that can be used to enhance and teach these skills. The varied opinions contained in each book examine many different aspects of a single issue. While examining these conveniently edited opposing views, readers can develop critical thinking skills such as the ability to compare and contrast authors' credibility, facts, argumentation styles, use of persuasive techniques, and other stylistic tools. In short, the Opposing Viewpoints Series is an ideal way to attain the higher-level thinking and reading skills so essential in a culture of diverse and contradictory opinions.

In addition to providing a tool for critical thinking, Opposing Viewpoints books challenge readers to question their own strongly held opinions and assumptions. Most people form their opinions on the basis of upbringing, peer pressure, and personal, cultural, or professional bias. By reading carefully balanced opposing views, readers must directly confront new ideas as well as the opinions of those with whom they disagree. This is not to simplistically argue that everyone who reads opposing views will—or should—change his or her opinion. Instead, the series enhances readers' understanding of their own views by encouraging confrontation with opposing ideas. Careful examination of others' views can lead to the readers' understanding of the logical inconsistencies in their own opinions, perspective on why they hold an opinion, and the consideration of the possibility that their opinion requires further evaluation.

Evaluating Other Opinions

To ensure that this type of examination occurs, Opposing Viewpoints books present all types of opinions. Prominent spokespeople on different sides of each issue as well as well-known professionals from many disciplines challenge the reader. An additional goal of the series is to provide a forum for other, less known, or even unpopular viewpoints. The opinion of an ordinary person who has had to make the decision to cut off life support from a terminally ill relative, for example, may be just as valuable and provide just as much insight as a medical ethicist's professional opinion. The editors have two additional purposes in including these less known views. One, the editors encourage readers to respect others' opinions—even when not enhanced by professional credibility. It is only by reading or listening to and objectively evaluating others' ideas that one can determine whether they are worthy of consideration. Two, the inclusion of such viewpoints encourages the important critical thinking skill of objectively evaluating an author's credentials and bias. This evaluation will illuminate an author's reasons for taking a particular stance on an issue and will aid in readers' evaluation of the author's ideas.

It is our hope that these books will give readers a deeper understanding of the issues debated and an appreciation of the complexity of even seemingly simple issues when good and honest people disagree. This awareness is particularly important in a democratic society such as ours in which people enter into public debate to determine the common good. Those with whom one disagrees should not be regarded as enemies but rather as people whose views deserve careful examination and may shed light on one's own.

Thomas Jefferson once said that "difference of opinion leads to inquiry, and inquiry to truth." Jefferson, a broadly educated man, argued that "if a nation expects to be ignorant and free . . . it expects what never was and never will be." As individuals and as a nation, it is imperative that we consider the opinions of others and examine them with skill and discernment. The Opposing Viewpoints Series is intended to help readers achieve this goal.

David L. Bender and Bruno Leone,
Founders

Greenhaven Press anthologies primarily consist of previously published material taken from a variety of sources, including periodicals, books, scholarly journals, newspapers, government documents, and position papers from private and public organizations. These original sources are often edited for length and to ensure their accessibility for a young adult audience. The anthology editors also change the original titles of these works in order to clearly present the main thesis of each viewpoint and to explicitly indicate the opinion presented in the viewpoint. These alterations are made in consideration of both the reading and comprehension levels of a young adult audience. Every effort is made to ensure that Greenhaven Press accurately reflects the original intent of the authors included in this anthology.

Introduction

"There has to be some form of punishment [for marijuana users]. If that means big fines and . . . jail time, absolutely."

—Brett Richardson, D.A.R.E. officer

"It makes little sense to send people to jail for using [marijuana, which] should be categorized somewhere between alcohol and tobacco on one hand and caffeine on the other."

—Richard Lowry, National Review editor

Since the 1600s Americans have cultivated *Cannabis sativa* L, an herb from which marijuana is produced. Useful in the manufacture of paper, clothing, and rope, the plant was legal tender in most colonies. In the twentieth century, however, attitudes toward marijuana altered significantly. After people discovered that cannabis produced psychoactive effects when smoked and began to use it recreationally, its reputation as a useful crop diminished. Criticized by some and praised by others, marijuana has undergone constant reassessment over the past century. As people's views of cannabis have swung wildly, from seeing it as an innocuous plant to a damaging drug and back again, so too have the laws that govern it, alternating between stringent and lenient. Ever-changing attitudes toward the drug's harmfulness, and shifting stereotypes about those who use it, explain why marijuana remains at the center of intense debate.

The first law restricting marijuana use was established in 1914. At that time Mexican immigrants were flowing into Texas. Rumors spread that the newcomers were cannabis addicts who provided the drug to children. Many Americans also believed that marijuana gave users superhuman strength and created uncontrollable, violent urges. At the time, the Texas state legislature reinforced the stereotype: "All Mexicans are crazy, and [marijuana] is what makes them crazy." Comments journalist Eric Schlosser, "Marijuana was depicted as an alien intrusion into American life, capable of transforming healthy teenagers into sex-crazed maniacs." Scholars believe that marijuana's harms and the prevalence of drug use among Mexicans were exaggerated in order to justify prejudice against immigrants. This anti-immigrant sentiment gave rise to an ordinance banning cannabis.

Other states began passing similar referenda, and soon a federal war against marijuana was started by Harry Anslinger, head of the Federal Bureau of Narcotics (FBN). Using "evil weed," he declared, led to murders and sex crimes, making marijuana use a law enforcement problem, not a public health issue. Judges were urged by Anslinger to "jail offenders, then throw away the key." Not surprisingly, Anslinger backed the 1937 Marihuana Tax Act, which criminalized possession of marijuana nationwide. By 1962 laws against marijuana use had become so strict that in some states someone convicted of a second offense for selling cannabis to minors could face the death penalty. Anslinger also created an FBN file containing reports on jazz musicians, who he believed used cannabis. Anslinger claimed, "Most marijuana smokers are Negroes, Hispanics, jazz musicians, and entertainers. Their satanic music is driven by marijuana."

With the dawn of the 1960s came a change in attitudes toward drug use. During this era people questioned and rebelled against authority, challenged stereotypes, and pushed for equal rights. Many young people began to doubt the validity of many commonly held beliefs about drugs, especially marijuana. Smoking cannabis, once an activity in which only fringe groups participated, became acceptable among many, and marijuana laws were relaxed. Schlosser contends,

> As marijuana use became widespread among white middle-class college students, there was a reappraisal of marijuana laws that for decades had imprisoned poor Mexicans and African Americans without much public dissent. Drug abuse policy shifted [to one] with more emphasis on treatment than on punishment.

Reflecting this view, a federal law reduced penalties for possession of small amounts of marijuana. To President Richard Nixon's dismay, his 1972 National Commission on Marijuana even declared that cannabis should be decriminalized for private use. Most states loosened their marijuana laws during the 1970s.

The public's view of marijuana shifted yet again, however, with the election of Ronald Reagan, who identified marijuana as America's most dangerous drug. In 1982 he announced, "We must mobilize all our forces to stop the flow of drugs into this country . . . to erase the false glamour that surrounds drugs, and to brand drugs such as marijuana exactly for what they are—dangerous." Upon being informed that one in twelve Americans smoked cannabis regularly, President Reagan launched a "just say no" antidrug campaign and created a post known as the drug czar. The drug czar's job is to coordinate the nation's drug control programs.

Once again marijuana became a criminal justice issue. Antidrug laws increased penalties for marijuana offenses. The 1986 Anti–Drug Abuse Act, for example, created mandatory minimum prison sentences for cannabis distributors, requiring judges to sentence them to set amounts of prison time without considering the circumstances of each case. Another act strengthened asset forfeiture laws, which allowed police to confiscate property and money that may have been obtained by or used in criminal activity. Now the Drug Enforcement Administration (DEA) could seize the assets of suspected marijuana traffickers who had not been charged or convicted of a crime due to lack of evidence.

Paradoxically, during this time the DEA's administrative law judge, Francis Young, announced that cannabis had medicinal value and a low potential for abuse. Accordingly, he recommended that the DEA ease restrictions on the drug, allowing it to be prescribed for medical use under controlled conditions. However, the DEA and others feared that this would imply that marijuana is safe. Public policy expert and marijuana activist Rick Doblin noted at the time,

> Parent and anti-drug groups and the International Association of Chiefs of Police have expressed concern about the 'signal value' of sanctioning marijuana's medical use. They fear medical use of marijuana might lead to increased experimentation by adolescents resulting in deleterious consequences.

Today many Americans maintain the view that marijuana is dangerous. Any use of the drug is illegal, and legislation governing it is rigid. Some states' zero tolerance laws, for instance, mandate felony charges for anyone caught with marijuana seeds. A backlash has occurred, though, fueled by citizens who feel the drug is fairly harmless and that strict cannabis policies have harmed too many lives. For decades approximately 75 percent of Americans supported the criminalization of cannabis for personal use, yet that number recently fell to 66 percent, indicating growing support for decriminalizing the drug.

After centuries of casual acceptance, marijuana wound up at the center of a political, social, and ideological controversy that continues to this day. Whether laws should prohibit marijuana use and how harshly violators should be punished are hotly debated in *Opposing Viewpoints: Marijuana* in the following chapters: Is Marijuana Use a Serious Problem? Are Current Marijuana Policies Effective and Fair? Should Marijuana Be Legalized? What Should Be Done to Limit Marijuana Use? It remains to be seen whether attitudes—and consequently, laws—will shift again as a result of this ongoing debate.

CHAPTER 1

Is Marijuana Use a Serious Problem?

Chapter Preface

According to the 2003 Monitoring the Future survey by the University of Michigan, 46 percent of high school seniors have tried marijuana. In addition, marijuana is the most widely used illegal drug among women of reproductive age. These statistics are alarming to doctors who believe the drug is harmful, particularly to anyone who wishes to have children. Cannabis, they claim, is detrimental to the reproductive systems of both males and females and to the unborn babies of pregnant women who use it. Marijuana advocates, on the other hand, insist that the drug is not damaging or that its harm is only temporary. Like many debates concerning the harmfulness of marijuana, the controversy over the drug's effects on reproduction has intensified as conflicting marijuana studies are published.

Cannabis may indeed be dangerous, according to the results of several studies. One animal study cited by PRIDE Surveys, which helps schools monitor student drug use, determined that in females, heavy use of marijuana interferes with signals that regulate hormones. As a result, menstrual cycles stop. Only after a woman abstains from the drug for several months does her cycle resume, the organization asserts. In males cannabis use decreases testosterone levels and sperm counts and even leads to infertility, PRIDE maintains. Philip Cohen of *New Scientist* reported that when scientists treated sperm with a chemical similar to the active ingredient in cannabis, the sperm's movement slowed and their ability to fertilize an egg became inhibited. "It really stops them cold," notes reproductive biologist Herbert Schuel.

Of even greater concern to most doctors are pregnant women who use marijuana. Whether and how their babies are affected is unclear since the results of marijuana studies are often conflicting. PRIDE states that cannabis use during pregnancy causes miscarriages and stillbirths. The babies who survive, it says, have subtle defects in their central nervous systems. "These babies show abnormal reactions to light and sound, exhibit tremors and startles, and have the high-pitched cry associated with drug withdrawal," PRIDE declares. The children may later develop learning disabilities, it adds. Even marijuana advocates such as Lester Grinspoon,

James B. Bakalar, and Ethan Russo concede that some babies suffer these types of birth defects when their mothers used marijuana heavily during pregnancy.

Other scientists, however, counter assertions that cannabis causes birth defects or other harmful conditions associated with reproduction. Susan Astley and her coworkers at the University of Washington, for instance, researched the occurrence of birth defects in babies of drug-using mothers and ultimately refuted assertions that marijuana causes birth defects. Some groups such as the National Organization for the Reform of Marijuana Laws (NORML) claim that pregnant women may even benefit from using marijuana. "While cannabis use is not recommended in pregnancy," the organization maintains, "it may be of medical value to some women in treating morning sickness or easing childbirth."

As for charges that marijuana decreases hormone levels, Grinspoon and his associates admit that some male users have low sperm counts and testosterone levels yet assert that the reduction is of little concern. Citing a Costa Rican study, they contend that regular smoking of marijuana does not affect males' masculine development. Moreover, they point out, "There is no evidence that the changes in sperm count and testosterone produced by marihuana affect sexual performance or fertility." NORML concurs: "Not a single case of impaired fertility has ever been observed in humans of either sex."

Other analysts altogether reject the view that marijuana affects sperm count or fertility. They charge that these claims stem from a 1974 study, and that subsequent research has failed to repeat its findings that frequent marijuana users had lower sperm counts than occasional users. "In fact," reads an article in *Trip Magazine*, "in a 1979 study, men spent thirty days in a closed lab smoking up to twenty marijuana cigarettes a day. When researchers examined their sperm counts, none were outside normal ranges."

Much controversy surrounds the question of marijuana's harmfulness. Making the debate especially confusing is the fact that there is evidence to support the arguments on both sides. In the following chapter authors tackle the question of whether marijuana is a serious problem.

> *"Marijuana use is associated with poor school performance, lower grades, less satisfaction with school, worse attitudes toward school, and poorer school attendance."*

Marijuana Use Is Harmful

Joseph M. Rey, Andres Martin, and Peter Krabman

Joseph M. Rey of the University of Sydney, Andres Martin of the Yale Child Study Center, and Peter Krabman of the Coral Tree Family Service in Australia contend that marijuana is dangerous and addictive, especially for youths. In the following viewpoint they present evidence that when adolescents use marijuana regularly, their IQ drops, and they may become unmotivated, drop out of school, and progress to other drug use. Anxiety disorders and depression may be attributed to marijuana use as well, they claim, and its use during adolescence increases the risk of psychotic illnesses such as schizophrenia.

As you read, consider the following questions:
1. What are three predictors of marijuana dependence, according to the authors?
2. What did Fergusson's and Horwood's study suggest about cannabis use?
3. What do the authors say may result when schizophrenics use cannabis?

Joseph M. Rey, Andres Martin, and Peter Krabman, "Is the Party Over? Cannabis and Juvenile Psychiatric Disorder: The Past 10 Years," *Journal of the American Academy of Child and Adolescent Psychiatry*, vol. 43, October 2004, p. 1,194.

At least 3% of 40-year-olds used marijuana daily in the United States in 2002, the same as the average rate of 12th graders who used marijuana more than 40 times in the past 30 days between 1967 and 2002. This suggests that there is a core of heavy marijuana users that may not have changed much in the past quarter century and that, in most cases, the habit may be already established by the time they finish high school.

Marijuana Dependence and Withdrawal

DSM [Diagnostic and Statistical Manual of Mental Disorders] IV does not list cannabis withdrawal as a disorder because its "clinical significance is uncertain" [according to the American Psychiatric Association]. Skeptics highlight that the [body's slow metabolization] of THC [marijuana's psychoactive ingredient] is not consistent with a withdrawal syndrome, which typically appears after a few hours. [Researcher A.J. Budney and his associates] assessed in their homes 12 daily marijuana users who did not use other illicit drugs on 16 consecutive days during which they smoked marijuana as usual, abstained from smoking, returned to smoking, and abstained again. Consumption of alcohol and nicotine was allowed. Irritability, restlessness, anger, and sleep problems increased significantly on cessation of use. This is consistent with other studies, reports by young people in residential care who were marijuana dependent, findings in community surveys, and laboratory studies. Thus, the symptoms and intensity of withdrawal in severe marijuana users appear clinically significant and are not dissimilar to those observed during nicotine withdrawal.

The concept of cannabis dependence has also been criticized. Contrary to this, the National Comorbidity Survey in the United States showed that 9% of those who ever used marijuana met DSM criteria for a lifetime diagnosis of dependence. In the Dutch Nemesis study, based on a sample of approximately 7,000 people aged 18 to 65, 10% of those who reported having used marijuana at least once met DSM criteria for cannabis dependence. In a large New Zealand birth cohort, 9% met DSM-IV criteria for dependence by the age of 21 years. These data suggest that approximately 1 in 10 people exposed to marijuana develops dependence, and the risk increases with frequency of use.

Who Becomes Dependent?

Genetic studies suggest that . . . there are moderate to substantial genetic influences and modest to moderate shared environmental influences on cannabis initiation, use, and problem use.

Cannabis use is more frequent among young people from socially disadvantaged backgrounds, with adverse childhood circumstances, with criminal or substance-using parents, with behavioral problems during childhood, who are prone to novelty seeking, [and] with friends involved in drug use and antisocial activities. Cigarette smoking, beginning to use marijuana before the age of 17 years, and weekly use are predictors of dependence, whereas lower education, lower socioeconomic status, and parental death before the age of 15 have been associated with early initiation. A prospective study showed that subjective responses to cannabis when adolescents were first exposed to the drug predict later risk of dependence: Those reporting five positive reactions had odds of later dependence that were more than 20 times higher than those who did not. This is consistent with the finding that electing to use cannabis in preference to alcohol may be an early sign of addiction, although cannabis may be preferred to alcohol in some populations.

Is Cannabis a Gateway Drug?

[In 1970 researcher L.N.] Robins [and coauthors] reported that early use of cannabis was associated with later heroin use. Subsequent studies have confirmed that youths who lived in the last third of the 20th century usually followed a sequence in their use of substances: from alcohol and tobacco to marijuana to other drugs such as cocaine and heroin. Several theories have been advanced to explain this phenomenon, which has significant clinical and policy implications and as such has generated much debate.

One theory is that there is a selective recruitment to cannabis use of adolescents with a tendency to use psychoactive substances with the sequence of use purely reflecting the availability of and access to these drugs. Statistical modeling using data derived from the National Household Survey of Drug Abuse including birth cohorts from 1964 through 1982 showed that a propensity to use psychoactive substances could reproduce all the drug use phenomena observed.

Handelsman. © 1993 by Tribune Media Services, Inc. Reproduced by permission.

Another explanation, the gateway hypothesis, states that using cannabis in some way facilitates the progression to using drugs such as cocaine and heroin. Analyzing data from a birth cohort of New Zealand children, [D.M.] Fergusson and [L.J.] Horwood [of the Christchurch School of Medicine & Health Sciences] showed that by age 21, nearly 70% had used marijuana and 26% had used other illicit drugs. In all but three cases, use of cannabis had preceded the use of other illicit drugs, and those using cannabis more than 50 times per year were 59 times more likely to use other illicit drugs. Progression to using other drugs was more likely with the earlier use of marijuana, independent of genetic factors. However, the strength of this association lessened with increasing age: strong at age 14 to 15 but weaker, although still significant, by age 20 to 21. These findings and those of other studies suggest that marijuana use is a factor in the progression to other drug use.

It is possible also that using cannabis and enjoying it may encourage experimentation with other illicit drugs or that the use of cannabis may place individuals in contact with drug-using subcultures that facilitate access to other illicit drugs. . . .

Cognitive Impairment

Numerous single-dose studies have shown that THC produces a dose-dependent reduction in performance on laboratory tasks measuring memory, attention, reaction time, and motor control. There is also growing evidence from experimental and epidemiological studies that recent marijuana use reduces driving ability and increases the risk of car crashes, particularly when drivers consume both alcohol and marijuana. However, most of the data (except about motor vehicle accidents, which includes adolescents) come from adult participants. Ascertaining whether long-term use results in chronic cognitive impairment has proven more difficult.

[Researcher P.A.] Fried [and associates] examined changes in IQ in a group of 70 young people aged 17 to 23 from a cohort followed prospectively and whose IQ before using cannabis was known. They concluded that IQ of participants who currently smoked five or more joints per week decreased by four points on average. A negative effect on IQ was not observed among participants who had been heavy users but were no longer using. One study reported that early-onset users (before age 17) differed significantly both from the late-onset users (at age 17 or later) and controls on verbal IQ, with those who started using earlier having a lower verbal IQ. However, most research has been performed on older, long-term users, the quality of the studies is generally poor (e.g., small groups, inadequate control of confounders), and some impairments may be preexisting. Findings can be summarized as showing that (1) gross cognitive impairment, as seen in heavy alcohol users, is not observed after quitting marijuana; (2) long-term users may show a small decrease in their ability to learn and remember new information (of limited clinical relevance); (3) it has not been demonstrated conclusively that long-term daily consumption results in persistent cognitive impairment after cessation of use.

Amotivational Syndrome and School Dropouts

There are considerable data showing that marijuana use is associated with poor school performance, lower grades, less satisfaction with school, worse attitudes toward school, and poorer school attendance. Cannabis use is also higher among school dropouts and is associated with later unemployment. There are several possible explanations for this. First, the performance at school of young students regularly intoxicated with marijuana may suffer due to the effects of intoxication. Second, regular use may cause an "amotivational syndrome" that may decrease participation in educational activities. Third, users may hold negative attitudes toward school, reinforced by affiliation with rebellious, drug-using peers. Finally, early use of cannabis may increase the likelihood of adopting adult roles prematurely through early sexual intercourse and teenage pregnancy.

Fergusson [and associates], using data gathered in the course of a 25-year longitudinal study of an unselected birth cohort of 1,265 children, reported that (1) adolescents who had used marijuana on at least 100 occasions until the age of 16 were 3.7 times more likely to leave school without qualifications than those who had not used; (2) participants using cannabis on at least 100 occasions by age 18 were just as likely to go to university as nonusers; (3) those using cannabis on at least 100 occasions by age 20 were just as likely to obtain a degree by age 25; (4) although later cannabis use was associated with a variety of adverse family and psychosocial circumstances, use was unrelated to levels of cognitive ability and academic achievement measured in middle childhood and early adolescence; (5) a reverse causal association (i.e., dropping out of school leading to higher use of cannabis) was unlikely. These results are consistent with those of . . . another prospective study but do not support the cognitive impairment or "amotivational syndrome" explanations. If that were the case, it would be expected that the effects of cannabis use on achievement would have become more marked with increasing age, while the opposite was true. Thus, adolescents who use marijuana

24

regularly are more likely to leave school without qualifications, but the effects of cannabis use on educational attainment once they complete high school are less clear.

Depression and Anxiety

The association between cannabis use, depression, and anxiety disorders has received little attention until recently. Panic attacks and other anxiety symptoms are common, particularly among female users, but there is a noteworthy lack of good data on the link between anxiety disorders and marijuana use.

It has been postulated that depressive symptoms may lead individuals to initiate and to persist using marijuana. Some suggested that cannabis has antidepressant activity, whereas others indicated that marijuana worsens depressive symptoms in depressed patients. Cross-sectional studies have shown an association between cannabis use and depressive symptoms in a representative sample of adolescents but not in adults. Cannabis use increased the risk of later DSM-III-R major depression fourfold in a 15-year follow-up of 1,920 adults in the United States. Follow-up of a community sample of 736 adults from upstate New York showed that earlier marijuana use predicted DSM-III-R major depressive disorder in the late 20s. [Researcher G.C.] Patton [and coworkers] followed 1,601 Australian secondary school students aged 14 to 15 for 7 years. Daily use in females was associated with a fivefold increase in the odds of reporting a syndrome of depression and anxiety at 21 years. Weekly or more frequent cannabis use doubled the risk. . . .

Cannabis and Psychosis

As many as 15% of cannabis users report psychotic symptoms after use. Many patients with schizophrenia use cannabis, and the association between cannabis and psychosis is well established. Can cannabis cause this condition, or do psychotic patients use cannabis for self-medication? The study often quoted in support of the causal hypothesis dates back to 1987. It examined the incidence of schizophrenia in more than 50,000 Swedish conscripts followed up for 15 years and showed that marijuana use during adolescence increased the risk of schizophrenia. Questions, however, remained about the validity of the diagnosis, the possible etiological role of other drugs, and whether arodromal [initial] symptoms [of psychosis] might have led to cannabis use rather than cannabis triggering the psychosis. More recent studies show that use of marijuana during adolescence increases the risk of psychotic illness in adulthood even after taking into account the effect of prodromal symptoms and other drug use. Further, these studies suggest that risk increases with the amount of marijuana consumed and with earlier onset of use. [L.J.] Phillips [and coresearchers] followed a group of 100 young people at "ultra high" risk of schizophrenia; 12 months later, one-third had become psychotic, but marijuana use did not increase the risk. These individuals already had some psychotic symptoms, which were used to identify them at ultra high risk. It is possible that, given the rapid progression to a full-blown psychosis, the effect of marijuana use was not important enough to influence the course of the illness.

Taken together, these studies seem to support the position that cannabis increases the risk of psychosis. They are inconsistent with the view that the association is due to self-medication. Further, risk appears to increase with length and intensity of cannabis use. These data largely refer to marijuana use during adolescence; it is possible that the effects of cannabis are different later in life.

On the basis of the above studies, [researcher Filip] Smit [and his associates] estimated that cannabis use doubled the risk of later schizophrenia (from 5 to 10 new cases per 10,000 person-years). If this were true, the increase in marijuana use in the past 50 years would have resulted in a substantial increase in the number of people with schizophrenia in many countries. [Louisa] Degenhardt [and her coresearchers] modeled this hypothesis on eight Australian birth cohorts from 1940 to 1979 but did not find evidence of an increase in the incidence of schizophrenia of the magnitude predicted. However, they did find support for the view that cannabis use may bring forward the onset of schizophrenia because persons born in more recent cohorts seem to have an earlier onset of the illness.

Cannabis also exacerbates the symptoms of schizophrenia. Marijuana users with schizophrenia have an earlier age at onset, more psychotic symptoms, a poorer response to antipsychotic drugs, and a worse outcome than people with schizophrenia who do not use. . . .

Early Cannabis Use Is Harmful

The weight of the data points in the direction of early and heavy use of cannabis having negative effects on youth psychosocial functioning and psychopathology. Further genetic studies, better understanding of the neurophysiology of THC, and qualitative research into the experiences of marijuana users and the ways in which cannabis use might shape life directions and choices will help to clarify the uncertainties.

Infrequent cannabis use causes few mental health or behavioral problems, but this does not mean that cannabis use is harmless. Clinicians have a role in making young people aware of the risks. It is hoped that as information on the hazards for mental health of cannabis use percolates high schools, perceptions of harmfulness may increase and use diminish. Although changes in perceptions of harmfulness of the drug among the young seem to be one of the factors driving the fluctuations in use, it is necessary to ascertain further the reasons for the ebbs and flows to guide prevention.

Evidence is accumulating that regular marijuana use during adolescence may have effects, whether biological, psychological, or social, that are different from those in later stages of development. Although there has been much discussion about the association between cannabis consumption and psychosis, research in the past 10 years has highlighted the link with depression. Most of the recent data are contrary to the view that marijuana is in some way used to self-medicate or to relieve psychotic or depressive symptoms. Practitioners should reject this myth—one that may get in the way of recognizing drug use problems and impede appropriate interventions.

> "*Researchers have compared heavy long-term cannabis users with nonusers and found no evidence of intellectual or neurological damage, no changes in personality, and no loss of the will to work.*"

Marijuana Use Is Not Usually Harmful

Lester Grinspoon, James B. Bakalar, and Ethan Russo

Lester Grinspoon is associate professor emeritus of psychiatry and James B. Bakalar is lecturer in law in the department of psychiatry at Harvard Medical School. Ethan Russo, a neurologist, founded the *Journal of Cannabis Therapeutics*. In the following viewpoint they argue that there is little evidence of tolerance and withdrawal in marijuana users; in fact, they assert, the drug is less addictive than alcohol or tobacco. In addition, the drug does not cause intellectual or neurological damage, personality changes, or a lack of motivation, they assert. They also refute the ideas that using marijuana leads to other drug use or incites violence.

As you read, consider the following questions:
1. How do the authors respond to suggestions that amotivational syndrome is related to inherent properties of marijuana?
2. What do Allentuck and Bowman conclude about cannabis psychosis?
3. What is the authors' objection to the Swedish schizophrenia study?

Lester Grinspoon, James B. Bakalar, and Ethan Russo, *Substance Abuse: A Comprehensive Textbook*. Philadelphia: Lippincott, Williams & Wilkins, 2004. Copyright © 2004 by Lippincott, Williams & Wilkins. Reproduced by permission of the publisher and the authors.

In recent years the psychological and physical effects of long-term use [of marihuana] have caused most concern. Studies are often conflicting and permit various views of marihuana's possible harmfulness. This complicates the task of presenting an objective statement about the issue.

One of the first questions asked about any drug is whether it is addictive or produces dependence. This question is hard to answer because the terms addiction and dependence have no agreed-upon definitions. Two recognized signs of addiction are tolerance and withdrawal symptoms; these are rarely a serious problem for marihuana users. In the early stages, they actually become more sensitive to the desired effects. After continued heavy use, some tolerance to both physiological and psychological effects develops, although it seems to vary considerably among individuals. Almost no one reports an urgent need to increase the dose to recapture the original sensation. What is called behavioral tolerance may be partly a matter of learning to compensate for the effects of high doses, and may explain why farm workers in some Third World countries are able to do heavy physical labor while smoking a great deal of marihuana.

A mild withdrawal reaction also occurs in animal experiments and possibly in some human beings who take high doses for a long time. The rarely reported mild symptoms are anxiety, insomnia, tremors, and chills, lasting for a day or two. It is unclear how common this reaction is; in a Jamaican study, heavy ganja [marihuana] users did not report abstinence symptoms when withdrawn from the drug. In any case, there is little evidence that the withdrawal reaction ordinarily presents serious problems to marihuana users or causes them to go on taking the drug. In a recent comprehensive review, cannabis withdrawal was seen as producing symptoms that were low-level to non-existent, with inconsistent onset and offset, with heterogeneous effects claimed with greatest support for transient agitation, appetite change and sleep disturbance. In sum, the concept of cannabis withdrawal was considered unproven.

In a more important sense, dependence means an unhealthy and often unwanted preoccupation with a drug to the exclusion of most other things. People suffering from drug dependence find that they are constantly thinking about the drug, or intoxicated, or recovering from its effects. The habit impairs their mental and physical health and hurts their work, family life, and friendships. They often know that they are using too much and repeatedly make unsuccessful attempts to cut down or stop. These problems seem to afflict proportionately fewer marihuana smokers than users of alcohol, tobacco, heroin, or cocaine. Even heavy users in places like Jamaica and Costa Rica do not seem to be dependent in this damaging sense. Marihuana's capacity to lead to psychological dependence is not as strong as that of either tobacco or alcohol. Two experts from the University of California, San Francisco and National Institute on Drug Abuse independently compared the dependency potential of cannabis, alcohol, nicotine, caffeine, cocaine and heroin. Cannabis was considered by both to carry the lowest overall risk.

It is often difficult to distinguish between drug use as a cause of problems and drug use as an effect; this is especially true in the case of marihuana. Most people who develop a dependency on marihuana would also be likely to develop other dependencies because of anxiety, depression, or feelings of inadequacy. The original condition is likely to matter more than the attempt to relieve it by means of the drug. The troubled teenager who smokes cannabis throughout the school day certainly has a problem, and excessive use of marihuana may be one of its symptoms.

Cognitive Effects and Amotivational Syndrome Are Unproven

The idea has persisted that in the long run smoking marihuana causes some sort of mental or emotional deterioration. In three major studies conducted in Jamaica, Costa Rica, and Greece, researchers have compared heavy long-term cannabis users with nonusers and found no evidence of intellectual or neurological damage, no changes in personality, and no loss of the will to work or participate in society. The Costa Rican study showed no difference between heavy users (seven or more marihuana cigarettes a day) and lighter users (six or fewer cigarettes a day). Experiments in the United States show no effects of fairly heavy marihuana use on learning, perception, or motivation over periods as long as a year.

On the other side are clinical reports of a personality change called the amotivational syndrome. Its symptoms are said to be passivity, aimlessness, apathy, uncommunicativeness, and lack of ambition. Some proposed explanations are hormone changes, brain damage, sedation, and depression. Since the amotivational syndrome does not seem to occur in Greek or Caribbean farm laborers, some writers suggest that it affects only skilled and educated people who need to do more complex thinking. However, there is no credible evidence that what is meant by this syndrome is related to any inherent properties of the drug rather than to different sociocultural adaptations on the part of the users.

The problem of distinguishing causes from symptoms is particularly acute here. Heavy drug users in our society are often bored, depressed, and listless, or alienated, cynical, and rebellious. Sometimes the drugs cause these states of mind and sometimes they result from personality characteristics that lead to drug abuse. Drug abuse can be an excuse for failure, or a form of self-medication. Because of these complications and the absence of confirmation from controlled studies, the existence of an amotivational syndrome caused by cannabis use has to be regarded as unproved.

No Evidence for the Gateway Hypothesis or Violence Theory

Much attention has also been devoted to the idea that marihuana smoking leads to the use of opiates and other illicit drugs: the stepping stone hypothesis, now commonly referred to as the gateway hypothesis, which has been rejected after extensive study by the Institute of Medicine and Canadian Senate. In this country, almost everyone who uses any other illicit drug has smoked marihuana first, just as almost everyone who smokes marihuana has drunk alcohol first. Anyone who uses any given drug is more likely to be interested in others, for some of the same reasons. People who use illicit drugs, in particular, are somewhat more likely to find themselves in company where other illicit drugs are available. None of this proves that using one drug leads to or causes the use of another. Most marihuana smokers do not use heroin or cocaine,

31

just as most alcohol drinkers do not use marihuana. The metaphor of stepping stones suggests that if no one smoked marihuana it would be more difficult for anyone to develop an interest in opiates or cocaine. There is no convincing evidence for or against this. What is clear is that at many times and places marihuana has been used without these drugs, and that these drugs have been used without marihuana.

Only the unsophisticated continue to believe that cannabis leads to violence and crime. Indeed, instead of inciting criminal behavior, cannabis may tend to suppress it. The intoxication induces a mild lethargy that is not conducive to any physical activity, let alone the commission of crimes. The release of inhibitions results in fantasy and verbal (rather than behavioral) expression. During the high, marihuana users may say and think things they would not ordinarily say and think, but they generally do not do things that are foreign to their nature. If they are not already criminals, they will not commit crimes under the influence of the drug. . . .

Cannabis Psychosis

A common assertion made about cannabis is that it may lead to psychosis. The literature on this subject is vast, and it divides into all shades of opinion. Many psychiatrists in India, Egypt, Morocco, and Nigeria have declared emphatically that the drug can produce insanity; others insist that it does not. One of the authorities most often quoted in support of the indictment is Benabud of Morocco. He believes that the drug produces a specific syndrome called "cannabis psychosis." His description of the identifying symptoms is far from clear, however, and other investigators dispute the existence of such a psychosis. The symptoms said to characterize this syndrome are also common to other acute toxic states, including, particularly in Morocco, those associated with malnutrition and endemic infections. Benabud estimates that the number of kif (marihuana) smokers suffering from all types of psychosis is not more than 5 in 1000; this rate, however, is lower than the estimated total prevalence of all psychoses in populations of other countries. One would have to assume either (a) that there is a much lower prevalence of psychoses other than cannabis psychosis among kif smokers in Morocco or (b) that there is no such thing as a cannabis psychosis and the drug is contributing little or nothing to the prevalence rate for psychoses.

[Psychiatrist Walter] Bromberg, in a report of one of his studies, listed 31 patients whose psychoses he attributed to the toxic effects of marihuana. Of these 31, however, 7 patients were already predisposed to functional psychoses that were only precipitated by the drug, 7 others were later found to be schizophrenics, and 1 was later diagnosed as a manic-depressive. The Chopras in India, in examinations of 1238 cannabis users, found only 13 to be psychotic, which is about the usual prevalence of psychosis in the total population in Western countries. In the LaGuardia study, 9 of 77 people who were studied intensively had a history of psychosis; however, this high rate could be attributed to the fact that all those studied were patients in hospitals or institutions. [S.] Allentuck and [K.M.] Bowman, the psychiatrists who examined this group, concluded that "marihuana will not produce psychosis de novo in a well-integrated, stable person.". . .

The Problem with Cannabis and Schizophrenia Studies

Our own clinical experience and that of others suggests that cannabis may precipitate exacerbations in the psychotic processes of some schizophrenic patients at a time when their illnesses are otherwise reasonably well-controlled with antipsychotic drugs. In these patients it is often difficult to determine whether the use of cannabis is simply a precipitant of the psychosis or whether it is an attempt to treat symptomatically the earliest perceptions of decompensation; needless to say, the two possibilities are not mutually exclusive. There is little support for the idea that cannabis contributes to the etiology of schizophrenia. And in one recently reported case, a 19-year-old schizophrenic woman was more successfully treated with cannabidiol (one of the cannabinoids in marihuana) than she had been with haloperidol.

A recent study from Sweden on schizophrenia is most suspect. The authors examined Swedish conscripts from 1969. This investigation seems to be an attempt to rehabilitate an extremely criticized study of the same cohort published in

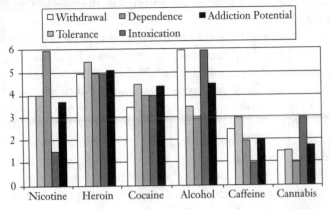

Addiction Ratings for Six Drugs

Legend: ☐ Withdrawal ▨ Dependence ■ Addiction Potential ▥ Tolerance ▩ Intoxication

Categories: Nicotine, Heroin, Cocaine, Alcohol, Caffeine, Cannabis

Adapted from P.J. Hilts, "Is Nicotine Addictive?" *New York Times*, August 2, 1994.

1987, which had been thoroughly criticized. In the current study, authors claim that based on their data, up to 13% of schizophrenia incidence could be attributable to cannabis. This is an unsubstantiated allegation, given that only 1.4% of the conscripts that ever smoked cannabis wound up schizophrenic. Men of such age are at the critical time of development of the disorder. All of the eventual schizophrenics in the earlier study were recognized to have some psychiatric issue before they entered the service! . . .

Anxiety Attacks Are Rare and Usually Mild

Some marihuana users suffer what are usually short-lived, acute, anxiety states, sometimes with and sometimes without accompanying paranoid thoughts. The anxiety may reach such proportions as properly to be called panic. Such panic reactions, although uncommon, probably constitute the most frequent adverse reaction to the moderate use of smoked marihuana. During this reaction, the sufferer may believe that the various distortions of bodily perceptions mean that he or she is dying or is undergoing some great physical catastrophe, and similarly the individual may interpret the psychological distortions induced by the drug as an indication of his or her loss of sanity. Panic states may, albeit rarely, be so severe as to incapacitate, usually for a relatively short period of time. The anxiety that characterizes the acute panic reaction resembles an attenuated version of the frightening parts of an LSD or other psychedelic experience[1]—the so-called "bad trip." Some proponents of the use of LSD in psychotherapy have asserted that the induced altered state of consciousness involves a lifting of repression. Although [this] . . . is questionable, many effects of LSD do suggest important alterations in ego defenses. These alterations presumably make new percepts and insights available to the ego; some, particularly those most directly derived from primary process, may be quite threatening, especially if there is no comfortable and supportive setting to facilitate the integration of the new awareness into the ego organization. Thus, psychedelic experiences may be accompanied by a great deal of anxiety, particularly when the drugs are taken under poor conditions of set and setting; to a much lesser extent, the same can be said of cannabis.

These reactions are self-limiting, and simple reassurance is the best method of treatment. Perhaps the main danger to the user is that she will be diagnosed as having a toxic psychosis [delirium that is usually temporary]. Users with this kind of reaction may be quite distressed, but they are not psychotic. The *sine qua non* of sanity, the ability to test reality, remains intact, and the panicked user is invariably able to relate the discomfort to the drug. There is no disorientation, nor are there true hallucinations. Sometimes this panic reaction is accompanied by paranoid ideation. The user may, for example, believe that the others in the room, especially if they are not well known, have some hostile intentions or that someone is going to inform on the user, often to the police, for smoking marihuana. Generally speaking, these paranoid ideas are not strongly held, and simple reassurance dispels them. . . .

Rarely, but especially among new users of marihuana, there occurs an acute depressive reaction. It is generally rather mild and transient but may sometimes require psychiatric intervention. This type of reaction is most likely to occur in a user who has some degree of underlying depression;

1. LSD and marihuana are both drugs that are generally classified as hallucinogens.

it is as though the drug allows the depression to be felt and experienced as such. Again, set and setting play an important part. Cannabis has been of benefit in mood stabilization in case reports from patients with bipolar disease.

Studies Have Found No Long-Term Physical Damage in Marihuana Users

Most recent research on the health hazards of marihuana concerns its long-term effects on the body. The main physiological effects of cannabis are increased appetite, a faster heartbeat, and slight reddening of the conjunctiva [eyes]. Although the increased heart rate could be a problem for people with cardiovascular disease, dangerous physical reactions to marihuana are almost unknown. No human being is known to have died of an overdose. By extrapolation from animal experiments, the ratio of lethal to effective (intoxicating) dose is estimated to be on the order of thousands to one.

Studies have examined the brain, the immune system, the reproductive system, and the lungs. Suggestions of long-term damage come almost exclusively from animal experiments and other laboratory work. Observations of marihuana users and the Caribbean, Greek, and other studies reveal little disease or organic pathology associated with the drug.

For example, there are several reports of damaged brain cells and changes in brain-wave readings in monkeys smoking marihuana, but neurological and neuropsychological tests in Greece, Jamaica, and Costa Rica found no evidence of functional brain damage.

"The troubling fact is that marijuana remains a pervasive and persistent presence in the lives of American teens."

Marijuana Use Among Youths Is a Serious Problem

National Center on Addiction and Substance Abuse at Columbia University

The National Center on Addiction and Substance Abuse at Columbia University (CASA) is a think tank that focuses on substance abuse. In the following excerpt it provides statistics to support its views that too many youths have tried marijuana, must enter marijuana treatment programs, and have been admitted to emergency rooms after using the drug. Studies conflict about whether marijuana use is increasing or decreasing, but CASA points out that due to survey methodology, marijuana use among young people is usually underestimated. Deterring use by teens is important, CASA states, because those who have never used marijuana by age twenty-one will most likely never use any drugs.

As you read, consider the following questions:
1. What does CASA say about proponents of marijuana decriminalization?
2. What two examples does CASA give to explain why youth may underreport their marijuana use?
3. According to the author, how many more teens have tried marijuana as compared to ecstasy or cocaine?

National Center on Addiction and Substance Abuse at Columbia University, *Non-Medical Marijuana II: Rite of Passage or Russian Roulette?* April 2004. Copyright © 2004 by The National Center on Addiction and Substance Abuse at Columbia University. Reproduced by permission.

From 1992 to 2001, the proportion of children and teenagers in treatment for marijuana dependence and abuse jumped 142 percent. From 1999 to 2002, emergency room admissions among 12- to 17-year-olds where marijuana was implicated jumped 48 percent. Evidence of a connection between the use of marijuana and the later use of other illegal drugs continues to accumulate, as does evidence of the adverse effects of marijuana on the brain, heart and lungs.

Against mounting indications of its dangers, marijuana remains a pervasive presence in the lives of American children and teens. That is why CASA [National Center on Addiction and Substance Abuse at Columbia University] decided to issue this White Paper with the most current information about non-medical marijuana. We seek to alert teenagers and their parents to the dangers of marijuana and curb teen use of the drug. The non-medical use of marijuana is a matter of special concern for teens and parents, since CASA's research has consistently found that an individual who gets through age 21 without using the drug is virtually certain never to use it or other illegal drugs. . . .

Mixed Messages

In 1999, CASA released the White Paper *Non-Medical Marijuana: Rite of Passage or Russian Roulette*, which described American marijuana policy and reviewed the likely consequences of marijuana legalization on the extent of use. CASA's 1999 White Paper concluded that proponents of decriminalization and legalization underestimate the role of the law in discouraging the number of users and frequency of use, and misperceive the dangers of marijuana use. This paper, *Non-Medical Marijuana II*, updates the 1999 White Paper and reports new findings about marijuana use and its consequences.

The message from national statistics on marijuana use by teens is somewhat mixed. The Monitoring the Future Study shows a downward trend in marijuana use among teenagers since 1999: in its 2003 survey, 46.1 percent of twelfth graders report that they have tried marijuana, compared with 49.7 percent in 1999. Tenth and eighth graders report similar declines. (Table 1.1)

Table 1.1 The Monitoring the Future Study, 1999–2003

Lifetime Marijuana Use Among 8th, 10th, and 12th Graders (by percent)

Grade	1999	2000	2001	2002	2003
12th	49.7	48.8	49.0	47.8	46.1
10th	40.9	40.3	40.1	38.7	36.4
8th	22.0	20.3	20.4	19.2	17.5

The message from the National Survey on Drug Use and Health (formerly the National Household Survey on Drug Abuse) on marijuana use by 12- to 17-year-olds is less clear. There is an upward trend in marijuana use among 12- to 17-year-olds, from 19.7 percent in 1999 to 20.6 percent in 2002; however, use among such teens decreased slightly between 2001 and 2002 (from 21.9 percent to 20.6 percent). (Table 1.2) It is not clear whether these differences are statistically significant, especially the decline from 2001 to 2002, since the National Survey on Drug Use and Health notes that methodological changes in the 2002 survey may make comparisons to past years unreliable.

Table 1.2 National Household Survey on Drug Abuse/National Survey on Drug Use and Health

Lifetime Marijuana Use Among 12- to 17-Year-Olds, 1999–2002 (by percent)

1999	2000	2001	2002
19.7	20.4	21.9	20.6

Marijuana Use Is Likely Underreported

In any case, both these surveys likely underestimate marijuana use among teenagers since they are based on self-reports of marijuana use. In self-report surveys, young people typically underreport their substance use. The National Survey on Drug Use and Health is based on personal interviews performed in a household and children are only interviewed when a parent is in the home, increasing the likelihood that the children will underreport risky behaviors such as substance use. The Monitoring the Future survey questionnaires are group administered in classrooms during a normal class period, reducing the likelihood that respondents will provide accurate answers to questionnaire items.

Whether or not teen marijuana use has declined and to what extent, the reality is that at least five million teens have tried marijuana, including almost half of high school seniors. Next to alcohol and tobacco, marijuana is the drug of choice for American teens. It is by far the most widely used illicit drug: about six times as many teens have tried marijuana as have tried Ecstasy or cocaine.

Teens Have Easy Access to Marijuana

Even if we take the optimistic view that marijuana use among children and teens is declining, the troubling fact is that marijuana remains a pervasive and persistent presence in the lives of American teens. In CASA's 2003 survey of 1,987 teens aged 12 to 17, 34 percent reported that marijuana was the easiest substance to buy (compared with cigarettes and beer), up from 27 percent in 1999.

Nearly 40 percent of teens—about 10 million—reported in 2003 that they could buy marijuana within a day; 20 percent could buy the drug within an hour. This measure of availability is down from 1999, when 44 percent of teens reported they could buy marijuana within a day and 30 percent could buy the drug within an hour.

Most people use marijuana for the first time when they are teenagers. Teenage initiates to the drug start using it at very young ages: among youths aged 12 to 17 who have ever tried marijuana, the mean age of initiation is 13 and a half. The mean age of initiation among adults aged 18 to 25 who have ever tried marijuana is 16.

With marijuana use among teens so common, the age of initiation so low and such large numbers of youngsters able to get the drug with relative ease, it is crucial that teens, parents, teachers and policymakers have the most up-to-date information about marijuana—including the drug's potency, its health consequences and other risks associated with its use, and that they understand the impact of teen and adult perceptions and attitudes about the drug on likelihood of use.

"*It is encouraging news that more American youths are getting the message that drugs are dangerous, including marijuana.*"

Marijuana Use Among Youths Is Declining

Substance Abuse and Mental Health Services Administration

In the following viewpoint the Substance Abuse and Mental Health Services Administration (SAMHSA) asserts that fewer youths are using marijuana, a decline which the agency attributes to President George W. Bush's efforts to prevent drug abuse and treat addicts. While marijuana is still the most commonly used illicit drug, SAMHSA maintains, more young people are aware of the drug's risks. In addition, SAMHSA notes, fewer youths are heavy users, and teens report that it has become more difficult to obtain marijuana. SAMHSA is part of the Department of Health and Human Services.

As you read, consider the following questions:
1. According to the viewpoint, what is Access to Recovery and what is it expected to do once it receives a budget increase?
2. What does SAMHSA say about the 2.6 million new marijuana users in 2002?
3. What happened to the rate of current marijuana users who were exposed to antidrug messages outside of school, in SAMHSA's contention?

Substance Abuse and Mental Health Services Administration, *Nation's Youth Turning Away from Marijuana, as Perceptions of Risk Rise*, September 10, 2004.

[D]epartment of Health and Human Services (HHS)] Secretary Tommy G. Thompson announced today [September 10, 2004] that there is a five percent decline in the number of American youth between the ages of 12 and 17 who have ever used marijuana. Current use of marijuana plummeted nearly 30 percent among 12- and 13-year-olds. The findings were included in the 2003 National Survey on Drug Use and Health released today at the annual Recovery Month press conference.

The findings, released by HHS' Substance Abuse and Mental Health Services Administration (SAMHSA), show that while overall, the change in the category "current use of any illicit drug" was not statistically significant, the use of some drugs decreased sharply. For youth [age] 12–17, past year use of Ecstasy and LSD dropped precipitously, by 41 percent for Ecstasy and 54 percent for LSD. Overall, 19.5 million Americans ages 12 and older, 8 percent of this population, currently use illicit drugs. The data indicate that of the 16.7 million adult users (18 and older) of illicit drugs in 2003, about 74 percent were employed either full time or part time.

Prevention and Treatment Efforts Are Working

"It is encouraging news that more American youths are getting the message that drugs are dangerous, including marijuana," Secretary Thompson said. "President [George W.] Bush recognizes that we as a nation must do more to ensure that our children don't use drugs in the first place and to help Americans get the treatment for alcohol and drug addiction that they need. That is why the President has invested significantly in drug abuse prevention and treatment programs. It's a cornerstone of his compassionate agenda."

President Bush's fiscal year 2005 budget request includes a 5 percent increase for substance abuse treatment, prevention and research, including a doubling of the funding for the Access to Recovery treatment program. President Bush is requesting $200 million for Access to Recovery, which provides vouchers to individuals to access drug- and alcohol-abuse treatment programs. With the doubling of the budget, Access to Recovery would help 100,000 people who want to obtain drug and alcohol treatment services but can't afford them.

"The prevention efforts of millions of parents, educators, and community leaders are working. Young people are getting the message that marijuana, which is substantially more potent today than it was 20 years ago, is a dangerous drug, and they are increasingly staying away from it," said John Walters, Director of National Drug Control Policy. "These new data reaffirm the critical roles parents and anti-drug advertising play in keeping our children safer, healthier, and drug-free."

Survey Finds Marijuana Use Is Decreasing

Marijuana use, which had been rising sharply in all three grades of secondary school during the early to mid-1990s, began to turn downward in 1997 among 8th graders and then did the same in 1998 among 10th and 12th graders. Only the 8th graders showed a continuation of this decline in 2000, however. In 2001, use remained level in all three grades. But since 2001, all three grades have shown a significant decline in their annual prevalence of marijuana use. . . .

Daily marijuana use rose substantially among secondary school and college students between 1992 and 2000 but somewhat less so among young adults. In 2001, the increase in daily use continued for the 10th graders and young adults but halted for the 8th graders, 12th graders, and college students. Since then the rates of daily use have declined among 8th and 10th graders.

Lloyd D. Johnston et al., *Monitoring the Future: National Survey Results on Drug Use, 1975–2003*, 2003.

SAMHSA Administrator Charles Curie said: "Employers who think alcohol and drug abuse will never be a problem in their workplace need to consider that more than three quarters of adults who have serious drug and or alcohol problems are employed. Encouraging employees to find help when they need it can result in fewer accidents and fewer workers absent on Monday morning. It may even save an employee's life, family, or job. Creating a drug-free workplace program or enhancing an existing program can lead to a healthier, more productive work force and be an important part of solving one of our nation's most persistent problems."

The survey found that of the 19.4 million adults (age 18 and over) characterized with abuse of or dependence on alcohol or drugs (19.4 million) in 2003, 14.9 million (77 percent) were employed either full or part time. This amounts to over ten percent of full-time workers as well as over ten percent of part-time workers.

Marijuana Use Is Declining Among Youth

Marijuana continues to be the most commonly used illicit drug, with 14.6 million current users (6.2 percent of the population). The study shows that there were an estimated 2.6 million new marijuana users in 2002. About two thirds of these new users were under age 18, and about half were female.

An important positive change detected by the survey was an increase in the perception of risk in using marijuana once a month or more frequently. Both youth and young adults reported a significant increase in their awareness of the risks of smoking marijuana. Particularly striking was the 20 percent decline between 2002 and 2003 in the number of youth that were "heavy users" of marijuana (those smoking either daily or 20 or more days per month). Perceived availability of the drug also declined significantly among youth.

The results of this year's survey demonstrate that anti-drug messages inside and outside of school, participation in religious and other activities, parental disapproval of substance use and positive attitudes about school are linked to lower rates of youth marijuana use. For example, those exposed to anti-drug messages outside of school had rates of current marijuana use that were 25 percent lower than those not reporting such exposure (7.5 percent vs. 10.0 percent). Youth who believe that their parents would "strongly disapprove" of marijuana had use rates fully 80 percent lower than those who reported that their parents would not "strongly disapprove" (5.4 percent vs. 28.7 percent).

*"Samples of marijuana testing at 9 percent
or higher THC . . . increased more than
600 percent from 1994 . . . to 2002."*

Marijuana Is Becoming More Potent

National Drug Intelligence Center

In the viewpoint that follows, the National Drug Intelligence Center (NDIC) contends that the average potency of marijuana has soared in recent years and that high-potency marijuana has become more available. Higher-potency marijuana can produce intense reactions, the organization asserts. In fact, the increased availability of higher-potency cannabis, the NDIC suggests, may be partly responsible for the rising number of emergency room visits where marijuana is involved and drug treatment admissions that have occurred since 1994. The NDIC, the nation's center for strategic domestic counterdrug intelligence, also produces drug threat assessments. This report combines information from enforcement and intelligence agencies with comments from the NDIC.

As you read, consider the following questions:
1. In NIDA's contention, what happens in the first hour after a person smokes marijuana?
2. Why don't all cannabis growers produce high-potent product, in the NDIC's view?
3. According to the author, what percentage of state and local law enforcement agencies reported that the availability of marijuana was high or moderate in 2004?

National Drug Intelligence Center, "National Drug Threat Assessment 2005," www.usdoj.gov, February 2005.

The escalating prevalence of higher potency marijuana such as sinsemilla has resulted in an increase in average marijuana potency; however, high potency marijuana constitutes a relatively small portion of the marijuana available throughout the United States. Commercial-grade marijuana is the most widely available type throughout the country.

Demand is higher for marijuana than for any other illicit drug; however, marijuana use among eighth, tenth, and twelfth graders as well as college students has declined since peaking in the late 1990s.

The consequences of marijuana use evidenced in ED [emergency department] mentions and treatment admissions have increased steadily over the last decade; however, three significant underlying factors should be considered when analyzing such increases. First, marijuana often is used with alcohol or other illicit drugs, which obscures the relevance of marijuana as a cause of many ED mentions. Second, a rise in treatment referrals through the criminal justice system has contributed largely to the increase in marijuana-related treatment admissions. Third, increased prevalence of higher potency marijuana has likely resulted in a greater number of individuals experiencing more intense and often unpleasant effects of the drug, leading them to seek medical intervention. . . .

Adverse Effects

Marijuana is not harmless. Marijuana's effects can include those problems attendant to cigarette smoking as well as problems with distorted perception and loss of coordination, which can contribute to household, occupational, or vehicular accidents. For example, in 2001 an estimated 38,000 U.S. high school seniors reported that they had crashed a vehicle while driving under the influence of marijuana. Other effects include problems with memory and learning, difficulty in thinking and problem solving, and increased heart rate. According to one study, fewer heavy users of marijuana completed college and more had household incomes of less than $30,000 as compared with a control group, despite similar educational and economic backgrounds. (In this study, heavy users smoked marijuana a mean of 18,000 times and no less than 5,000 times, while control group subjects smoked at least once but no more than 50 times in their life.) NIDA [National Institute on Drug Abuse] reports that another study has indicated that a user's heart attack risk quadruples in the first hour after smoking marijuana. . . .

Highly Potent Marijuana

The escalating prevalence of higher potency marijuana such as sinsemilla appears to have resulted in an increase in average potency levels. Samples of marijuana testing at 9 percent or higher THC (delta-9-tetrahydrocannabinol) [the active chemical in marijuana] increased more than 600 percent from 1994 (104 of 3,281 samples) to 2002 (545 of 2,378 samples), according to data from the Potency Monitoring Project. Yet the increase in the average potency of tested marijuana and sinsemilla during that period was less dramatic. Average THC levels for both types rose approximately 50 percent, from 3.50 to 5.11 percent THC for marijuana and from 7.49 to 11.43 percent THC for sinsemilla.

NDIC Comment: Marijuana potency has increased; however, it is unlikely that average potency levels will reach 20 or 30 percent THC in the near term. Even with the advances in indoor cultivation techniques or marijuana production methods used throughout the United States and Canada where much of the higher potency marijuana is produced, THC levels remain, typically, under 15 percent. Growers can and do produce marijuana with potency levels over 20 percent; however, not all growers have the capability or the determination either to produce top-quality marijuana or to achieve the highest potential yield from their crops. The trend toward larger grows controlled by organized crime groups in Canada and, to a lesser extent, in the United States should help stabilize or further slow the rise in average potency levels. The interests of DTOs [drug trafficking organizations] and criminal groups are in marijuana's profitability, and they are unlikely to invest the care required to mass-produce top-quality marijuana, particularly in the drying, manicuring, and curing stages of production. Thus, average THC levels likely will continue to increase only gradually or remain relatively stable.

Marijuana-Related Emergencies and Treatment Admissions

The consequences of marijuana use evidenced in ED mentions and treatment admissions have increased steadily over the last decade. Marijuana-related ED mentions increased nearly 200 percent from 1994 to 2002. Marijuana-related treatment admissions increased 100 percent during the same period.

NDIC Comment: The dramatic increases in marijuana-related ED mentions and treatment admissions often are viewed with concern, and while these increases may be attributable in part to the higher potency marijuana available today, this hypothesis has yet to be confirmed. Polydrug use and integrating treatment services in the disposition of minor cases of marijuana possession are two significant underlying factors to consider when assessing the consequences of marijuana use. Marijuana very often is used sequentially or concurrently with alcohol or other illicit drugs. In fact, only 28 percent of marijuana-related ED episodes in 2002 involved marijuana alone, so the presence of alcohol or other illicit drugs undoubtedly obscures the relevance of marijuana as a cause of many ED visits. Also, a rise in treatment referrals through the criminal justice system (such as through drug courts begun in the early 1990s) has contributed largely to the increase in marijuana-related treatment admissions. According to SAMHSA [Substance Abuse and Mental Health Services Administration], treatment admissions referred by the criminal justice system were more likely to report marijuana as a primary substance of abuse than admissions referred by all other sources (24% vs. 10%). This is not to suggest that marijuana use is not harmful or that providing treatment as an alternative to arrest is a flawed policy, but these underlying factors do have bearing on analysis of marijuana's consequences. . . .

Availability of High-Potency Marijuana

All DEA [Drug Enforcement Administration] Field Divisions and HIDTA [High Intensity Drug Trafficking Areas] offices report that marijuana is readily, widely, or the most available illicit drug in their areas. Reports of increased availability largely concerned higher potency or Canadian Bud (also referred to as BC [British Columbia] Bud) marijuana reported by Field Divisions and HIDTA offices whose jurisdictions include the northern half of the country. Such reporting likely implicates Canadian marijuana, although higher potency marijuana is produced domestically, particularly in the Pacific Region, and the term Canadian Bud has been used to identify any marijuana consisting of buds and is not necessarily an accurate indicator of the country of origin. Areas where increased marijuana availability was identified include Detroit, North Dakota, South Dakota, Oregon, Washington, New Hampshire, Vermont, Colorado, Utah, Montana, and Wyoming. There were no reports of a trend toward decreased availability, although DEA Newark [New Jersey] attributed a recent shortage in marijuana supplies to law enforcement actions in late 2003.

Table 1. Average THC Concentration (in Percent) by Year Confiscated, 1994–2002

	1994	1996	1998	2000	2002
Marijuana	3.50	3.87	4.21	4.68	5.11
Sinsemilla	7.49	9.23	12.33	12.71	11.43

Potency Monitoring Project.

NDTS [National Drug Threat Survey] 2004 data show that 97.8 percent of state and local law enforcement agencies describe the availability of marijuana as high or moderate, little deviating from the percentages reported for 2003 (98.2%) and 2002 (96.9%). The percentage of agencies reporting high or moderate availability in 2004 ranged narrowly from a low of 97.1 percent in the Southeast to a high of 99.5 percent in the West. Although law enforcement agencies throughout the country identify marijuana as the most prevalent illicit drug in their areas, few consider it a significant threat to public health and safety, hence its relatively low ranking as the greatest drug threat.

Another indication that marijuana's availability is not declining is that federal seizures of marijuana have increased slightly overall since 2001. . . . However, while marijuana seizures have increased, the amounts seized over the 4-year period [2000–2003] have not varied significantly, nor has the location of most federal seizures. FDSS [Federal-Wide Drug Seizure System] data show that from 2000 to 2003, seizures in the four border states of Texas, Arizona, California, and New Mexico accounted for an average of 92 percent of all marijuana seized through incidents in which federal agencies participated. In 2004 seizures in Texas and Arizona alone accounted for 76 percent of total federal marijuana seizures.

The Demand for Higher-Potency Marijuana

Contrary to reports of increased availability and amounts seized, marijuana-related arrests have been declining, probably reflecting law enforcement's focus on more socially disruptive drugs, such as methamphetamine or crack, as well as the challenges posed by state and local laws inconsistent with federal laws governing marijuana. For example, the number of DEA arrests that involved marijuana declined overall from 7,096 in 2000 to 4,655 in 2003. At least 80 percent of DEA marijuana-related arrests in each year from 2000 through 2003 involved marijuana of foreign origin.

Potency levels reflect less the actual supply of marijuana available than they do the quality available. Thus the documented rise in marijuana potency (see Table 1) is more a factor of the availability of and demand for better quality marijuana. For example, according to data from the Potency Monitoring Project at the University of Mississippi, 23 percent of submitted samples tested at 9.0 percent THC or higher in 2002, compared with just 3 percent in 1994 (when some 900 more samples were tested than in 2002). The data also illustrate that despite advances in cultivation techniques that make it possible to produce marijuana with THC levels of 20 to 30 percent, yields of this strength are not the rule, and high potency marijuana—whether sinsemilla from Canada or the United States—more typically tests between 10 and 15 percent THC.

> "*Pot is better, just not the 30 times better that [national drug czar John] Walters cites. . . . Walters is disingenuously comparing the best pot of today with the worst of yesterday.*"

Claims That Marijuana Is Becoming More Potent Are Exaggerated

Daniel Forbes

Daniel Forbes claims in the following viewpoint that national drug czar John Walters's assertion that marijuana potency has increased by as much as thirty times is a gross distortion. Walters ignores the most current studies on marijuana potency, Forbes argues. Furthermore, by comparing the worst quality marijuana of the 1970s to the highest quality product of today, Walters is misrepresenting the facts, Forbes maintains. Forbes also points out that few people, especially adolescents, have access to the high potency marijuana to which Walters refers. Daniel Forbes has testified before the Senate and the House about drug-related issues.

As you read, consider the following questions:
1. In the author's contention, why does John Walters cite potency statistics from 1999?
2. What reasons does Forbes give to support his claim that the potency of sinsemilla is irrelevant?
3. According to Forbes, what happened after Walters's potency claims jumped from 7 percent to 14 percent?

M arijuana lost big on Election Day [2002]. Nevada's pot legalization proposal took only 39 percent of the vote. An Arizona decriminalization initiative did little better with 43 percent. And a mere 33 percent of Ohioans voted for a measure to treat instead of incarcerate minor drug offenders.

One reason for the ballot-box failure may have been the full-throttle, anti-marijuana campaign tour by White House Drug Czar John P. Walters. Walters, whose official title is director of the Office of National Drug Control Policy [ONDCP], inveighed against the demon weed in campaign swings through Ohio, Arizona, and Nevada (twice). At the heart of Walters' sermon: "It is not your father's marijuana." Today's users, he claims, confront pot that's up to 30 times stronger than what aging baby boomers smoked.

John Walters' Assertions Conflict with Government Figures

In an early September [2002] op-ed in the *San Francisco Chronicle*, Walters wrote: "In 1974, the average THC content of marijuana was less than 1 percent. But by 1999, potency averaged 7 percent." This is plain wrong. According to the federal government's own Potency Monitoring Project at the University of Mississippi, 1999's average was 4.56 percent. Referring to Walters' 7 percent figure, Dr. Mahmoud A. ElSohly, who runs the project, says, "That's not correct for an overall average." (THC is tetrahydrocannabinol, the active ingredient in pot.)

Walters also wrote that the THC level in "today's sinsemilla . . . averages 14 percent and ranges as high as 30 percent." (Sinsemilla is the highest-quality pot.) He concluded, "The point is that the potency of available marijuana has not merely 'doubled,' but increased as much as 30 times."

A couple of weeks later in the *Detroit News*, Walters gave even more alarming numbers about regular pot, claiming that "today's marijuana is 10 to 14 percent [THC]. And hybrids go up to 30 percent and above."

Walters' figures are grossly distorted. For starters, his figures for "today's sinsemilla" actually come from 1999. He ignores data from 2000 and 2001. That's presumably because sinsemilla potency spiked in 1999 at 13.38 percent (which, incidentally, rounds off to 13 percent *not* 14 percent). But the most recent full-year figure available, 2001, shows a potency of 9.55 percent. Yes, sinsemilla's THC count has been increasing, but its average over the past decade [from 1992 to 2002] is only 9.79 percent. More important, the potency of sinsemilla has little to do with quotidian reality for most pot-smokers. Sinsemilla comprises only 4.3 percent of the University of Mississippi's sample over the years. It's prohibitively expensive for casual (and young) users: On the East Coast, the very best stuff is $700 an ounce.

The pot that most people, especially most kids, smoke is nowhere near as powerful as sinsemilla: The THC content of all pot last year was 5.32 percent; during the past decade, it averaged 4.1 percent. In other words, the marijuana that most kids smoke is about 5 percent THC—not 14 percent and certainly not 30 percent.

Comparing Apples and Oranges

As to Walters' claim that all those '70s hippies were getting goofy on the 1-percent stuff—basis for his 30-fold increase claim—the number lacks credibility. No one smokes 1-percent dope, at least not more than once. You make rope with it. The industrial hemp initiative approved by state election officials in South Dakota this year defined psychoactively worthless hemp as a plant with a "THC content of 1 percent or less."

Avowed marijuana enthusiast Keith Stroup, head of the National Organization for the Reform of Marijuana Laws, says: "One percent is not smokeable. That's really industrial hemp or ditchweed left over from World War II. All you'll get from that is a headache." In fact, in its formal reports, the Potency Monitoring Project even refers to 1-percent marijuana as "ditchweed." And in *Understanding Marijuana*, Mitch Earleywine, a University of Southern California psychology professor, writes, "Cannabis with this little THC has no impact on subjective experience."

Pot is better, just not the 30 times better that Walters cites to scare today's voters. Walters is disingenuously comparing the best pot of today with the worst of yesterday, rather than comparing average marijuana of a generation ago with average marijuana now. He's ginning up the figures he wants by contrasting stuff you might line your cat's litter box with to the alleged 30-percent pot—the likes of which a lucky (or rich) smoker might encounter once every several years.

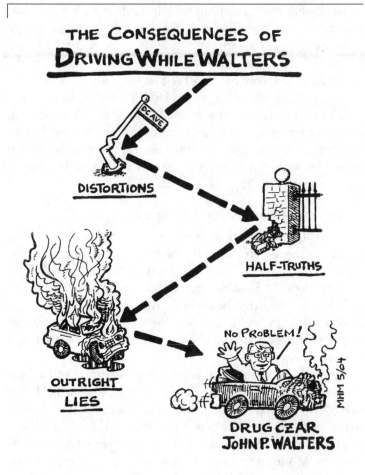

THE CONSEQUENCES OF
DRIVING WHILE WALTERS

DISTORTIONS

HALF-TRUTHS

OUTRIGHT LIES

NO PROBLEM!

DRUG CZAR
JOHN P. WALTERS

Nor are Walters' fudged figures consistent from day to day or even consistent with what his own office says. Now he's talking a 30-fold increase, but just last May [2001], Walters wrote in a *Washington Post* op-ed that pot is "10 to 20 times stronger" than it was a generation ago. (He made his more modest claim before news broke of the legalization push in Nevada and before he started his heavy campaigning.)

ONDCP contradicted the boss's 30-fold nonsense in its own anti-drug media campaign, which features an essay titled, "Kids and Marijuana: The Facts." It states that THC levels "rose from under 2 percent in the late 1970s and early 1980s to just over 6 percent in 2000." (It was actually never under 2 percent in the '80s and was 4.88 percent, not 6 percent, in 2000, but hey—close enough for government work.)

Scare Tactics

Those minor exaggerations aside, such were "The Facts" when I checked the ONDCP site this fall. But as the campaign season heated up, and Walters' potency claims jumped from 7 percent to October's superpot of 10 percent and 14 percent, these "facts" faded away. The ONDCP essay now states simply: "Today's marijuana is more potent and its effects can be more intense."

The original ONDCP "Facts" correspond with estimates from UCLA professor Mark Kleiman that marijuana has roughly tripled in potency. Kleiman also notes that there is no evidence at all that marijuana is getting kids more stoned than it used to. Writing on his own blog, Kleiman cites the respected annual University of Michigan study that asks respondents about levels of intoxication. Writes Kleiman: "The line for marijuana is flat as a pancake. Kids who get stoned today aren't getting any more stoned than their parents were. That ought to be the end of the argument." Kleiman points out that the average joint is now half its former size, so even if kids are smoking more powerful pot, they are smoking less of it. "'Not your father's pot' is a great way to convince [boomer parents] to ignore their own experience, personal or vicarious, and believe what they are told to believe."

Of course, the Walters scare campaign is nothing new. Back in 1994, City University of New York professor and marijuana advocate John Morgan cited three *New York Times* articles warning of alarming increases in marijuana's potency. They were published in 1980, 1986, and 1994.

> *"An estimated 38,000 . . . students reported in 2001 that they crashed while driving under the influence of marijuana."*

Driving Under the Influence of Marijuana Is Dangerous

Part I: Office of National Drug Control Policy
Part II: Stephen G. Wallace

Driving after using marijuana is risky, argue the authors of the following two-part viewpoint. In part I the Office of National Drug Control Policy (ONDCP) claims that the drug affects concentration, judgment, and coordination. The ONDCP, which establishes policies, priorities, and objectives for the nation's drug control program, has launched a campaign to deter marijuana use and encourage sober driving. In part II Stephen G. Wallace, the chairman and CEO of Students Against Destructive Decisions, declares that teens are misinformed about the perils of driving under the influence of marijuana. Wallace claims its use causes tens of thousands of car crashes, injuries, and deaths each year.

As you read, consider the following questions:

1. What does Norman Y. Mineta say is particularly dangerous about teens driving under the influence of marijuana, according to the ONDCP?
2. In the ONDCP's opinion, what three factors are associated with less-risky teen behavior?
3. What three main misconceptions does Wallace say teens have about driving under the influence of cannabis?

Part I: Office of National Drug Control Policy, "Recent Analysis Shows That One in Six High School Seniors Admitted Driving While High," www.whitehousedrug policy.gov, September 16, 2003. Part II: Stephen G. Wallace, "The Phantom Menace: Drugging and Driving Poses Threat to Teens During Summer Season," www.theantidrug.com, 2002.

I

Approximately one in six high school seniors in the United States admitted driving under the influence of marijuana, according to a recent analysis of Monitoring the Future data, and 41 percent of teens surveyed by SADD [Students Against Destructive Decisions]/Liberty Mutual said they were not concerned about driving after using drugs. Today [September 16, 2003] the nation's Drug Czar and Secretary of Transportation were joined by SADD, GEICO [an auto insurer], Mitsubishi Motors North America, and several driving safety leaders to steer teens clear of pot as they prepare to take on the responsibility of driving. Television advertisements to raise public awareness of the problem of drugged driving will run during the months of September and October [2003].

"Today's teens have gotten the wrong message about marijuana," said [drug czar] John P. Walters, Director of National Drug Control Policy. "Marijuana is harmful and can lead to risky decisions, such as driving while high or riding with drivers who are impaired. We want to encourage parents of new drivers to use this milestone in their teen's life to discuss the dangers of marijuana and being responsible behind the wheel."

"The Bush Administration is committed to the safety of all Americans," said Secretary Norman Y. Mineta. "Teens already have the highest crash risk of any age group, making traffic crashes the leading cause of death for young people age 15–20. Combining drug use with teens' inexperience on the road and risk-taking behavior is a recipe for disaster."

The Dangers of Driving Under Marijuana's Influence

The "Drugged Driving" short report released today from the National Survey on Drug Use and Health shows that, in 2002, between 10 and 18 percent of young drivers age 17 to 21 reported driving under the influence of an illicit drug during the past year. Driving-age teens (age 16–19) are also four times more likely to use marijuana than younger adolescents (age 12–15).

Estimates based on Monitoring the Future and Census Bureau data also show that of the nearly 4 million high school seniors in the United States, approximately one in six (600,000) drive under the influence of marijuana, a number nearly equivalent to those who drive under the influence of alcohol (640,000). Additionally, an estimated 38,000 of these students reported in 2001 that they crashed while driving under the influence of marijuana and 46,000 reported that they crashed while driving under the influence of alcohol.

A Study Tests the Driving Abilities of People Under the Influence of Cannabis

Cannabis significantly affected one criterion, known as tracking ability. Volunteers found it more difficult to hold a constant speed and follow the middle of the road accurately while driving around a figure-of-eight loop. . . . This test requires drivers to hold their concentration for a short time, a task which is particularly badly affected by the intoxicating effects of cannabis.

Arran Frood, "Dope at the Wheel," *New Scientist*, March 23, 2002.

Marijuana affects concentration, perception, coordination, and reaction time, many of the skills required for safe driving and other tasks. These effects can last up to 24 hours after smoking marijuana. Marijuana use can also make it difficult to judge distances and react to signals and sounds on the road.

Teens are high-risk drivers and have the highest crash risk of any age group. Nearly one in five 16-year-old drivers is involved in a collision in his or her first year of driving, making motor vehicle crashes the leading cause of death for young people age 15 to 20.

What Can Be Done?

Greater parent involvement, clear rules, and parental supervision are associated with less risky teen behavior, such as marijuana use and driving while high or under the influence of alcohol. Crashes were one-seventh less likely to occur among teens with strong parental monitoring, according to the *Journal of Safety Research*.

The National Youth Anti-Drug Media Campaign will raise public awareness on the issues of drugged driving and the harmful effects of teen marijuana use through the promotion of free Steer Clear of Pot materials; new Web content on www.TheAntiDrug.com and www.Freevibe.com; a new drivers' safety kit for teens and parents; advertisements on television with drugged driving messages; and partnerships with GEICO, the Department of Transportation, SADD, American Association of Motor Vehicle Administrators (AAMVA), American Driver & Traffic Safety Education Association (ADTSEA), Mitsubishi Motors North America, Liberty Mutual, and others to distribute drugged driving and marijuana prevention materials to drivers' education teachers, teens, and parents.

II

"Summer's lease hath all too short a date," wrote William Shakespeare, apparently foreshadowing the all-too-soon approach of fall. But a short summer season is time enough still for even the most unlikely of kids to find trouble in the most likely of places: cars and roadways. Two consecutive reports from the National Highway Traffic Safety Administration (NHTSA) make clear the devastating spike in teen fatalities during June, July and August.

With adult attention focused squarely on the dangers of teen drinking and driving (at least among those adults who bother to focus on such matters at all), another—and seemingly more common—threat to adolescent safety remains largely hidden and often difficult to detect: drugging and driving.

Misconceptions About Marijuana

As if rampant pot smoking by teens weren't problem enough, many of them believe that driving under the influence of cannabis poses little risk of impaired operation and virtually no chance of arrest. And that's bad news heading into one of the most dangerous times of year for young drivers.

"There's definitely a misconception that you can still drive under the influence of pot—that that's what differentiates pot from alcohol," a Massachusetts teen told me the other day, mirroring a prevalent view among youth that drugging and driving is a safe alternative to drinking and driving.

Let's look at the facts: Marijuana use, even a little, negatively affects driving performance and is linked to tens of thousands of serious automobile crashes, injuries and deaths each year. Marijuana and cars make for a combustible mix, blurring judgment and inviting catastrophe.

Even so, data from a 2002 survey of middle and high school students conducted by SADD (Students Against Destructive Decisions/Students Against Driving Drunk) and Liberty Mutual Group reveals that:

- At least one in three 7th–12th graders has used or is using drugs (36 percent);
- The majority of licensed teen drivers who use drugs regularly also drug and drive (68 percent);
- Among teens, driving after drugging is more prevalent (68 percent of those who use drugs regularly) than is driving after drinking (47 percent of those who drink regularly);
- More than one third of teens who are using drugs regularly are not concerned about riding in a car with a driver who is using drugs (38 percent).

Scary. So why is no one talking about this?

First, a preponderance of parents is unaware of the degree to which their teens have access to—and use—drugs.

Second, many parents who are aware seem unconcerned, perhaps underestimating the potency of today's weed (estimated to be 10–20 times stronger than the marijuana of yesteryear) or the possible consequences of its use.

But driving is only the quickest route to drug-induced disaster. Marijuana is, in fact, addictive and, much like alcohol and other drugs, it directly affects the brain, impairing the ability of young people to think, learn and grow . . . and all of this at a time when significant cognitive reorganization is taking place. In addition, clinicians observing kids on pot note increased apathy, loss of ambition, diminished ability to pursue long-term plans and a decline in school performance.

Marijuana is also used by more than a few teens to avoid dealing with, or to mask, important emotions brought about by a lot of "first time" situations, thus deferring problem solving and delaying healthy emotional development.

"The impairment in driving skills does not appear to be severe, even immediately after taking cannabis. . . . People . . . compensate for their impairment by taking fewer risks and driving more slowly."

Driving Under the Influence of Marijuana Is Not Especially Dangerous

National Organization for the Reform of Marijuana Laws

The National Organization for the Reform of Marijuana Laws (NORML) argues in the following viewpoint that marijuana has only a mild effect on psychomotor skills and does not play a significant role in vehicle crashes. Drivers under the influence of marijuana are safer than those who have been drinking alcohol, NORML asserts. According to the group and the research it cites, marijuana users are aware of their slight impairment, and thus decrease their driving speed and focus their attention more keenly on the road. While NORML does not advocate driving under the influence of marijuana, it suggests that the drug does not impair users significantly. NORML aims to reform state and federal marijuana laws and to ultimately legalize the drug.

As you read, consider the following questions:

1. According to NORML, what behaviors are exhibited by drivers under the influence of alcohol?
2. What three conclusions of the Bates and Blakely study are listed in the viewpoint?

It is well established that alcohol increases accident risk. Evidence of marijuana's culpability in on-road driving accidents is much less convincing.

Although cannabis intoxication has been shown to mildly impair psychomotor skills, this impairment does not appear to be severe or long lasting. In driving simulator tests, this impairment is typically manifested by subjects decreasing their driving speed and requiring greater time to respond to emergency situations.

Nevertheless, this impairment does not appear to play a significant role in on-road traffic accidents. A 2002 review of seven separate studies involving 7,934 drivers reported, "Crash culpability studies have failed to demonstrate that drivers with cannabinoids in the blood are significantly more likely than drug-free drivers to be culpable in road crashes." This result is likely because subjects under the influence of marijuana are aware of their impairment and compensate for it accordingly, such as by slowing down and by focusing their attention when they know a response will be required. This reaction is just the opposite of that exhibited by drivers under the influence of alcohol, who tend to drive in a more risky manner proportional to their intoxication.

Today, a large body of research exists exploring the impact of marijuana on psychomotor skills and actual driving performance. This research consists of driving simulator studies, on-road performance studies, crash culpability studies, and summary reviews of the existing evidence. To date, the result of this research is fairly consistent: Marijuana has a measurable yet relatively mild effect on psychomotor skills, yet it does not appear to play a significant role in vehicle crashes, particularly when compared to alcohol. [This] is a summary of some of the existing data.

(For more information on NORML's position regarding marijuana, driving and the law, please [read] NORML's Principles of Responsible Cannabis Use.)

Summaries of Auto Accident Research

"At the present time, the evidence to suggest an involvement of cannabis in road crashes is scientifically unproven.

To date . . . , seven studies using culpability analysis have been reported, involving a total of 7,934 drivers. Alcohol was detected as the only drug in 1,785 drivers, and together with cannabis in 390 drivers. Cannabis was detected in 684 drivers, and in 294 of these it was the only drug detected.

. . . *The results to date of crash culpability studies have failed to demonstrate that drivers with cannabinoids in the blood are significantly more likely than drug-free drivers to be culpable in road crashes.* . . . [When] cases in which THC [marijuana's psychoactive ingredient] was the only drug present were analyzed, the culpability ratio was found to be not significantly different from the no-drug group."

REFERENCE: G. Chesher and M. Longo. 2002. "Cannabis and alcohol in motor vehicle accidents."

"Cannabis leads to a more cautious style of driving, [but] it has a negative impact on decision time and trajectory. [However,] this in itself does not mean that drivers under the influence of cannabis represent a traffic safety risk. . . . *Cannabis alone, particularly in low doses, has little effect on the skills involved in automobile driving.*"

REFERENCE: Canadian Senate Special Committee on Illegal Drugs. 2002. *Cannabis: Summary Report: Our Position for a Canadian Public Policy.*

"This report has summarized available research on cannabis and driving.

. . . Evidence of impairment from the consumption of cannabis has been reported by studies using laboratory tests, driving simulators and on-road observation. . . . Both simulation and road trials generally find that driving behavior shortly after consumption of larger doses of cannabis results in (i) a more cautious driving style; (ii) increased variability in lane position (and headway); and (iii) longer decision times. *Whereas these results indicate a 'change' from normal conditions, they do not necessarily reflect 'impairment' in terms of performance effectiveness since few studies report increased accident risk.*"

REFERENCE: UK Department of Environment, Transport and the Regions (Road Safety Division). 2000. *Cannabis and Driving: A Review of the Literature and Commentary.*

"Overall, we conclude that the weight of the evidence indicates that:

1. *There is no evidence that consumption of cannabis alone increases the risk of culpability for traffic crash fatalities or injuries for which hospitalization occurs, and may reduce those risks.*
2. The evidence concerning the combined effect of cannabis and alcohol on the risk of traffic fatalities and injuries, relative to the risk of alcohol alone, is unclear.
3. It is not possible to exclude the possibility that the use of cannabis (with or without alcohol) leads to an increased risk of road traffic crashes causing less serious injuries and vehicle damage."

REFERENCE: M. Bates and T. Blakely. 1999. "Role of cannabis in motor vehicle crashes."

Drivers Compensate for Impairment Caused by Cannabis

"In conclusion, marijuana impairs driving behavior. *However, this impairment is mitigated in that subjects under marijuana treatment appear to perceive that they are indeed impaired.* Where they can compensate, they do, for example by not overtaking, by slowing down and by focusing their attention when they know a response will be required. . . . Effects on driving behavior are present up to an hour after smoking but do not continue for extended periods.

With respect to comparisons between alcohol and marijuana effects, these substances tend to differ in their effects. *In contrast to the compensatory behavior exhibited by subjects under marijuana treatment, subjects who have received alcohol tend to drive in a more risky manner. Both substances impair performance; however, the more cautious behavior of subjects who have received marijuana decreases the impact of the drug on performance, whereas the opposite holds true for alcohol.*"

REFERENCE: A. Smiley. 1999. "Marijuana: On-Road and Driving-Simulator Studies."

"Intoxication with cannabis leads to a slight impairment of psychomotor . . . function. . . . [However,] *the impairment in driving skills does not appear to be severe, even immediately after*

A Marijuana Smoker Speaks Out

Regular smoking of cannabis does not seem to have impaired my judgment when it comes to driving. I enjoy driving while high. I like to point out that I have driven many miles over the last 20 years without a single accident or even speeding ticket. My last vehicle, a 1983 Tercel wagon, was retired with a rusted out frame and over 400,000 accident-free kilometers on it and I was high for most of those km's [kilometers]. Driving while high causes me to drive a little slower and more attentively. I feel more attuned to my car and my surroundings. I'm also less prone to road rage and much more patient and courteous if I'm high.

Paul DeFelice, "How I Use Pot," Dr. Lester Grinspoon's Marijuana Uses. www.marijuana-uses.com.

---

taking cannabis, when subjects are tested in a driving simulator. This may be because people intoxicated by cannabis appear to compensate for their impairment by taking fewer risks and driving more slowly, whereas alcohol tends to encourage people to take great risks and drive more aggressively."

REFERENCE: UK House of Lords Select Committee on Science and Technology. 1998. *Ninth Report.*

"The evidence suggests that marijuana presents a real, but secondary safety risk; and that alcohol is the leading drug-related accident risk factor."

REFERENCES: D. Gieringer. 1988. "Marijuana, driving, and accident safety."

Researchers Believe Alcohol, Not Marijuana, Is Responsible for Serious Crashes

"For each of 2,500 injured drivers [who visited] a hospital, a blood sample was collected for later analysis.

There was a clear relationship between alcohol and culpability. . . . *In contrast, there was no significant increase in culpability for cannabinoids alone. While a relatively large number of injured drivers tested positive for cannabinoids, culpability rates were no higher than those for the drug free group.* This is consistent with other findings."

REFERENCE: Logan, M.C., Hunter, C.E., Lokan, R.J., White, J.M., & White, M.A. (2000). *The Prevalence of Alcohol,*

Cannabinoids, Benzodiazepines and Stimulants Amongst Injured Drivers and Their Role in Driver Culpability: Part II: The Relationship Between Drug Prevalence and Drug Concentration, and Driver Culpability.

"Blood samples from 894 patients presenting to two Emergency Departments for treatment of motor vehicle injur[ies] . . . were tested for alcohol and other drugs.

. . . Based on alcohol and drug testing of the full range of patients . . . alcohol is clearly the major drug associated with serious crashes and greater injury. *Patients testing positive for illicit drugs (marijuana, opiates, and cocaine), in the absence of alcohol, were in crashes very similar to those of patients with neither alcohol nor drugs. When other relevant variables were considered, these drugs were not associated with more severe crashes or greater injury.*"

REFERENCE: P. Waller et al. 1997. "Crash characteristics and injuries of victims impaired by alcohol versus illicit drugs."

"Blood specimens were collected from a sample of 1,882 drivers from 7 states, during 14 months in the years 1990 and 1991. The sample comprised operators of passenger cars, trucks, and motorcycles who died within 4 hours of their crash.

. . . While cannabinoids were detected in 7 percent of the drivers, the psychoactive agent THC was found in only 4 percent. . . . *The THC-only drivers had a responsibility rate below that of the drugfree drivers. . . . While the difference was not statistically significant, there was no indication that cannabis by itself was a cause of fatal crashes.*"

REFERENCE: K. Terhune. 1992. *The incidence and role of drugs in fatally injured drivers.*

Driving Performance Studies Find Marijuana Impairment Is Slight

"Marijuana's effects on actual driving performance were assessed in a series of three studies wherein dose-effect relationships were measured in actual driving situations that progressively approached reality.

... THC's effects on road-tracking ... never exceeded alcohol's ... and, were in no way unusual compared to many medicinal drugs. Yet, THC's effects differ qualitatively from many other drugs, especially alcohol. *Evidence from the present and previous studies strongly suggests that alcohol encourages risky driving whereas THC encourages greater caution, at least in experiments. Another way, THC seems to differ qualitatively from many other drugs is that the former's users seem better able to compensate for its adverse effects while driving under the influence."*

REFERENCE: H. Robbe. 1995. "Marijuana's effects on actual driving performance."

"This report concerns the effects of marijuana smoking on actual driving performance. ... This program of research has shown that marijuana, when taken alone, produces a moderate degree of driving impairment which is related to consumed THC dose. *The impairment manifests itself mainly in the ability to maintain a lateral position on the road, but its magnitude is not exceptional in comparison with changes produced by many medicinal drugs and alcohol. Drivers under the influence of marijuana retain insight in their performance and will compensate when they can, for example, by slowing down or increasing effort. As a consequence, THC's adverse effects on driving performance appear relatively small."*

REFERENCE: W. Hindrik and J. Robbe and J. O'Hanlon. 1993. *Marijuana and actual driving performance.*

"Overall, it is possible to conclude that cannabis has a measurable effect on psychomotor performance, particularly tracking ability. Its effect on higher cognitive functions, for example divided attention tasks associated with driving, appear not to be as critical. *Drivers under the influence of cannabis seem aware that they are impaired, and attempt to compensate for this impairment by reducing the difficulty of the driving task, for example by driving more slowly. ...*"

REFERENCE: B. Sexton et al. 2000. *The influence of cannabis on driving: A report prepared for the UK Department of the Environment. Transport and the Regions (Road Safety Division).*

Periodical Bibliography

The following articles have been selected to supplement the diverse views presented in this chapter.

Paul Armentano	"Cruising on Cannabis: Putting the Breaks on Doped Driving Misconceptions," National Organization for the Reform of Marijuana Laws, February 6, 2004. www.norml.org.
Brian C. Bennett	"Assessing the Marijuana 'Gateway' Theory," *BBSNews—In Black and White*, January 15, 2003. www.bbsnews.net.
Scott M. Burns	"An Open Letter to America's Prosecutors," Office of National Drug Control Policy, November 1, 2002. www.whitehousedrug policy.gov.
Philip Cohen	"Go Slow," *New Scientist*, December 12, 2000.
Drug Enforcement Administration	"Exposing the Myth of Medical Marijuana." www.dea.gov.
Drug Policy Alliance	"Drugged Driving." www.drugpolicy.org.
Ed Friedlander	"The Case Against Marijuana: A Pathologist's Perspective." www.pathguy.com.
Kathryn Lee	"Marijuana Use and Academic Achievement," *Sociological Perspectives*, Spring 2004.
National Institute on Drug Abuse	"InfoFacts: Marijuana," March 2004. www.nida.nih.gov.
National Organization for the Reform of Marijuana Laws	"Your Government Is Lying to You (Again) About Marijuana." www.norml.org.
National Survey on Drug Use and Health	"Marijuana Use and Delinquent Behaviors Among Youth," *NSDUH Report*, January 9, 2004.
Office of National Drug Control Policy	"What Americans Need to Know About Marijuana." www.whitehousedrugpolicy.gov.
Parents. The Anti-Drug	"Marijuana and Learning Fact Sheet," 2004. www.theantidrug.com.
PRIDE Surveys	"PRIDE Questionnaire Report for Grades 6–12: 2002–2003. PRIDE Surveys National Summary/Monthly Marijuana Users," August 29, 2003. www.pridesurveys.com.

CHAPTER 2

Are Current Marijuana Policies Effective and Fair?

Chapter Preface

Voting is an essential right in a democracy. Yet some Americans—currently 2 to 4 million of them—have forfeited their right to vote by committing and being convicted of a felony. Many people assert that anyone who commits a felony, which includes crimes such as murder and rape, should not participate in their country's democratic process. However, when the crime is a marijuana offense, considered a felony in many states, numerous citizens take a different stance. Whereas drugs like heroin and methamphetamine are widely considered to be dangerous and addictive, marijuana is frequently viewed as relatively harmless. In consequence, felony disenfranchisement laws are often seen as too harsh on marijuana offenders.

State laws restricting felons' voting rights vary widely. In two states felons may vote while incarcerated, whereas six states permanently ban ex-felons from casting votes. In seven states certain felony offenders can petition for their voting rights through a clemency process. The Right to Vote campaign aims to educate felons about this process. Its supporters maintain that voting is a cornerstone of democracy, one everyone—including marijuana users and dealers—should have the right to exercise.

Some commentators believe marijuana does less social harm than other drugs and do not see why people convicted of using it should lose the right to vote. Moreover, they assert, allowing people convicted of marijuana offenses to cast ballots facilitates their rehabilitation by helping them feel a sense of obligation to society. Mark Mauer of the Sentencing Project contends, "The more we can encourage that, the more likely people will want to respect the laws of that community." Critics of felony disenfranchisement laws maintain that the right to vote should be restored to ex-felons because they have already paid their debt to society.

Defenders of felon voting restrictions, on the other hand, insist that people who use marijuana are endangering themselves and society. Many feel that someone who harms society by committing a crime should not be allowed to shape the community's laws and choose its leaders. State representative Kent Grusendorf, who sought to bar ex-felons from voting unless they had been pardoned, believes the Right to Vote campaign is ridiculous. In questioning its mission to restore voting rights to current felons as well as ex-offenders, he asks, "So the basic principle of democracy is that you ought to let jailbirds vote?"

More importantly, supporters of felony disenfranchisement laws claim, the restrictions are necessary to protect the public. An 1884 Alabama court ruling, they point out, declares that the laws are designed not to punish ex-felons but "to preserve the purity of the ballot box." If allowed to vote, they fear, felons who violated marijuana laws might support propositions that would help them pursue illicit interests or would weaken law enforcement, such as proposals to legalize marijuana or to limit federal agents' power to investigate suspected marijuana dealers. Echoing this concern is the Heritage Foundation's Todd Gaziano, who states that felon voting "could have a perverse effect on the ability of law abiding citizens to reduce the deadly and debilitating crime in their communities."

The debate over whether or not marijuana offenders should have voting rights is shaped by views on marijuana's harmfulness. Those who see cannabis as hazardous tend to support strict laws governing its use and generally agree that those convicted of marijuana offenses should not be allowed to vote. Those who view the drug as benign usually support more relaxed marijuana laws that do not bar marijuana offenders from voting. The authors in the following chapter examine existing marijuana laws, questioning their efficacy and fairness.

"Arresting, let alone jailing, people for using [marijuana] seems outrageously disproportionate."

The War on Drugs Punishes Marijuana Users Too Harshly

Richard Lowry

National Review editor Richard Lowry maintains in the following selection that U.S. cannabis policies are too austere, resulting in unnecessarily punitive sentences for marijuana users. According to Lowry, state and federal laws mandate arrests, drug treatment programs, and even jail sentences for marijuana use or possession. These punishments are outrageous, in his opinion, because cannabis is far less harmful and less addictive than legal drugs such as alcohol or tobacco. Support of marijuana prohibition, he avers, is based on illogical circular arguments and long-standing cultural prejudice.

As you read, consider the following questions:
1. What point does Lowry make about drug prohibitionist James Q. Wilson?
2. According to the author, what are the drug warriors' two circular arguments?
3. What is marijuana's main danger to others and how should it be dealt with, in Lowry's view?

Rarely do trial balloons burst so quickly. During the [2001] British campaign, Tory shadow home secretary Ann Widdecombe had no sooner proposed tougher penalties for marijuana possession than a third of her fellow Tory shadow-cabinet ministers admitted to past marijuana use. Widdecombe immediately had to back off. The controversy reflected a split in the party, with the confessors attempting to embarrass Widdecombe politically. But something deeper was at work as well: a nascent attempt to reckon honestly with a drug that has been widely used by baby boomers and their generational successors, a tentative step toward a squaring by the political class of its personal experience with the drastic government rhetoric and policies regarding marijuana.

The American debate hasn't yet reached such a juncture, even though [the 2000] presidential campaign featured one candidate [George W. Bush] who pointedly refused to answer questions about his past drug use and another who—according to [Al] Gore biographer Bill Turque—spent much of his young adulthood smoking dope and skipping through fields of clover (and still managed to become one of the most notoriously uptight and ambitious politicians in the country). In recent years, the debate over marijuana policy has centered on the question of whether the drug should be available for medicinal purposes (Richard Brookhiser has written eloquently in NR [*National Review*] on the topic). Drug warriors call medical marijuana the camel's nose under the tent for legalization, and so—for many of its advocates—it is. Both sides in the medical-marijuana controversy have ulterior motives, which suggests it may be time to stop debating the nose and move on to the full camel.

We're All Liberalizers

Already, there has been some action. About a dozen states have passed medical-marijuana laws in recent years, and California voters, last November [2000], approved Proposition 36, mandating treatment instead of criminal penalties for all first- and second-time nonviolent drug offenders. Proponents of the initiative plan to export it to Ohio, Michigan, and Florida. Most such liberalization measures fare well at the polls—California's passed with 61 percent of the vote—

Judge Thelton Henderson on Marijuana Sentencing Laws

I'm opposed to mandatory minimums, in general, because I think they're unduly harsh. I think that they don't allow the judge the discretion to deal with individual problems. There is a formula that says you've been involved with a certain amount of drugs, for example, ergo you get the mandatory minimum. . . .

I think to best understand how the mandatory minimum works, you have to understand how the sentencing guidelines themselves work, and it's essentially a two-step process. . . . First, you assess the criminal off the offense level. And the offense level takes into account the amount of money . . . [and] the amount of drugs involved. You sort of add them up and then you take into account the person's criminal history. . . .

When those two elements are sufficiently large, it kicks you over into mandatory minimums. It's that simple, so that at a certain level, the offense level and the criminal history dictate a mandatory minimum of ten years in many cases, or perhaps twenty years in other cases. . . .

I had a fairly recent experience of two young men, up in Eureka, which is one of California's popular marijuana growing regions, and they were both in their twenties, and had a marijuana growing operation on a patch of land, and they both came up with a mandatory minimum of ten years. . . .

I felt awful. I still remember vividly, here are two young men who look like the kids next door. Not that that gets you off going to jail, but I felt awful because they're in the prime of life. I thought the sentence was much too harsh.

I thought, if I had discretion, I would have sentenced them to something much less, because I thought that they . . . were sufficiently remorseful. I think they could have learned their lesson with something closer to two years, perhaps three years.

Thelton Henderson, interviewed by PBS Frontline, *Busted: America's War on Marijuana*, Winter 1997–1998. www.pbs.org.

---

as long as they aren't perceived as going too far. Loosen, but don't legalize, seems to be the general public attitude, even as almost every politician still fears departing from [former drug czar] Bill Bennett orthodoxy on the issue. But listen carefully to the drug warriors, and you can hear some of them quietly reading marijuana out of the drug war. James Q. Wilson, for instance, perhaps the nation's most convincing advocate for drug prohibition, is careful to set marijuana aside from his arguments about the potentially ruinous effects of legalizing drugs.

There is good reason for this, since it makes little sense to send people to jail for using a drug that, in terms of its harmfulness, should be categorized somewhere between alcohol and tobacco on one hand and caffeine on the other. According to common estimates, alcohol and tobacco kill hundreds of thousands of people a year. In contrast, there is as a practical matter no such thing as a lethal overdose of marijuana. Yet federal law makes possessing a single joint punishable by up to a year in prison, and many states have similar penalties. There are about 700,000 marijuana arrests in the United States every year, roughly 80 percent for possession. Drug warriors have a strange relationship with these laws: They dispute the idea that anyone ever actually goes to prison for mere possession, but at the same time resist any suggestion that laws providing for exactly that should be struck from the books. So, in the end, one of the drug warriors' strongest arguments is that the laws they favor aren't enforced—we're all liberalizers now.

There has, of course, been a barrage of government-sponsored anti-marijuana propaganda over the last two decades, but the essential facts are clear: Marijuana is widely used, and for the vast majority of its users is nearly harmless and represents a temporary experiment or enthusiasm. A 1999 report by the Institute of Medicine—a highly credible outfit that is part of the National Academy of Sciences— found that "in 1996, 68.6 million people—32% of the U.S. population over 12 years old—had tried marijuana or hashish at least once in their lifetime, but only 5% were current users." The academic literature talks of "maturing out" of marijuana use the same way college kids grow out of backpacks and [philosopher Frederick] Nietzsche. Most marijuana users are between the ages of 18 and 25, and use plummets after age 34, by which time children and mortgages have blunted the appeal of rolling paper and bongs. . . .

Circular Arguments and Cultural Prejudice

[One] arrow in the drug warriors' quiver is the number of people being treated for marijuana: If the drug is so innocuous, why do they seek, or need, treatment? Drug warriors cite figures that say that roughly 100,000 people enter drug-treatment programs every year primarily for marijuana use. But often, the punishment for getting busted for marijuana possession is treatment. According to one government study, in 1998 54 percent of people in state-run treatment programs for marijuana were sent there by the criminal-justice system. So, there is a circularity here: The drug war mandates marijuana treatment, then its advocates point to the fact of that treatment to justify the drug war. Also, people who test positive in employment urine tests often have to get treatment to keep their jobs, and panicked parents will often deliver their marijuana-smoking sons and daughters to treatment programs. This is not to deny that there is such a thing as marijuana dependence. According to *The Lancet*, "About one in ten of those who ever use cannabis become dependent on it at some time during their 4 or 5 years of heaviest use.". . .

A small minority of people who smoke it may—by choice, as much as any addictive compulsion—eventually smoke enough of it for a long enough period of time to suffer impairments so subtle that they may not affect everyday functioning or be permanent. Arresting, let alone jailing, people for using such a drug seems outrageously disproportionate, which is why drug warriors are always so eager to deny that anyone ever goes to prison for it.

In this contention, the drug warriors are largely right. The fact is that the current regime is really only a half-step away from decriminalization. And despite all the heated rhetoric of the drug war, on marijuana there is a quasi-consensus: Legalizers think that marijuana laws shouldn't be on the books; prohibitionists think, in effect, that they shouldn't be enforced. A reasonable compromise would be a version of the Dutch model of decriminalization, removing criminal penalties for personal use of marijuana, but keeping the prohibition on street-trafficking and mass cultivation. . . .

Drug warriors, of course, will have none of it. They support a drug-war . . . doctrine under which no drug-war excess can ever be turned back—once a harsh law is on the books for marijuana possession, there it must remain lest the wrong "signal" be sent. "Drug use," as Bill Bennett has said, "is dangerous and immoral." But for the overwhelming majority of its users marijuana is not the least bit dangerous. (Marijuana's chief potential danger to others—its users driving while high—should, needless to say, continue to be treated as harshly as drunk driving.) As for the immorality of marijuana's use, it generally is immoral to break the law. But this is just another drug-war circularity: The marijuana laws create the occasion for this particular immorality. If it is on the basis of its effect—namely, intoxication—that Bennett considers marijuana immoral, then he has to explain why it's different from drunkenness, and why this particular sense of well-being should be banned in an America that is now the great mood-altering nation, with millions of people on Prozac and other drugs meant primarily to make them feel good.

In the end, marijuana prohibition basically relies on cultural prejudice. This is no small thing. Cultural prejudices are important. Alcohol and tobacco are woven into the very fabric of America. Marijuana doesn't have the equivalent of, say, the "brewer-patriot" Samuel Adams (its enthusiasts try to enlist George Washington, but he *grew* hemp instead of smoking it). Marijuana is an Eastern drug, and importantly for conservatives, many of its advocates over the years have looked and thought like [Beat poet] Allen Ginsberg. But that isn't much of an argument for keeping it illegal, and if marijuana started out culturally alien, it certainly isn't anymore.

> "*We should not capitulate in our war on drugs any more than we should surrender in our war on terrorism.*"

The War on Drugs Is Necessary to Reduce Marijuana Use

William J. Bennett

In the following viewpoint William J. Bennett cites the rising number of youths who use marijuana as evidence for the need to continue the war on drugs. Bennett contends that drug legalization efforts must be stopped or drug use, particularly among young people, will continue to rise. The war on drugs, he asserts, demands moral resolve and vigilance, not capitulation. William J. Bennett was the first director of the Office of National Drug Control Policy.

As you read, consider the following questions:
1. What does Bennett say results from the increasing potency of marijuana?
2. How would Proposition 203 "give the patina of official endorsement of marijuana use," in the author's contention?
3. According to Bennett, what other war depends on the war on drugs?

P oll numbers in support of softer drug laws are trending up, according to [the November 4, 2002] *Time Magazine* cover story. While only 34 percent of voters favor the complete legalization of marijuana, increasing majorities would support reducing penalties for possession and permitting the use of pot for medicinal purposes. That's the result of a relentless campaign to legalize drugs, funded by billionaire George Soros and others.

What *Time* does not report, however, are other numbers on the rise: the number of young people who currently use marijuana, the number of young initiates, the number seeking treatment for marijuana abuse, and the potency of today's marijuana.

Marijuana Use Is a Growing Problem

This fall [2002] we learned from the National Household Survey on Drug Abuse that one out of every ten young people (10.8 percent) age 12–17 was a current drug user in 2001, a 1.1 percent increase since 2000. Of these, 74 percent were reporting current marijuana use. The percentage of 16- to 17-year-olds reporting current marijuana use rose from 13.7 percent in 2000 to 14.9 percent in 2001. Among those age 18–25, current marijuana users increased from 13.6 percent in 2000 to 16.0 percent in 2001.

More young people are initiating marijuana use at an earlier age. The number seeking treatment for marijuana abuse is rising as well. Between 1992 and 1999, the number of adolescent marijuana treatment admissions rose 260 percent, according to the federal agency tracking drug abuse treatment statistics.

While marijuana is more prevalent, it is also more potent. The content of the active ingredient, THC, has increased from an average of less than one percent in 1974 to an average of seven percent today, and in some varieties ranging as high as 14 to 30 percent. This dramatic increase creates tolerance for lower doses, causing users to need higher doses to get the same effect.

Drug legalization proponents have distracted the public from these hard facts about illicit drugs. They have exploited public sympathy for those suffering from debilitating illnesses by proposing medical marijuana usage—itself a dubious proposition. But this fall [2002], their tactics reveal more about their true agenda. On three states' ballots this November, the push is to decrease penalties for possession of marijuana unrelated to any medical condition.

Teens Who Have Ever Used Marijuana

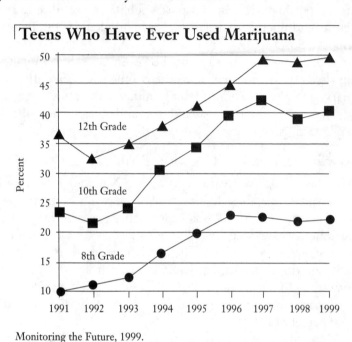

Monitoring the Future, 1999.

In Arizona, Proposition 203 would decriminalize possession of up to two ounces of marijuana, eliminate mandatory minimum sentences and require parole for those convicted of personal possession of a controlled substance. Even worse, it would give the patina of official endorsement of marijuana use by requiring the Department of Public Safety to be the distributor of marijuana from seized stashes.

In Nevada, Question 9 would decriminalize possession of up to three ounces of marijuana and set up a state-regulated system for growing and selling marijuana.

In Ohio, voters are being offered a false choice between incarceration and treatment. Ohio's Issue 1 would mandate substance abuse treatment for non-violent offenders but would stipulate no provision for testing people sentenced to treatment for compliance with the program.[1]

The numbers are not on the side of the drug legalization movement in Nevada and Ohio, where the pro-drug initiatives are falling behind in the polls. The drug legalizers' efforts look strongest in Arizona—oddly, where the proposal is most absurd. This calls attention to the need to be clear about the political agenda behind their efforts. Equivocations about drug legalization have clouded the public's thinking.

The War on Drugs Should Not Be Abandoned

We should not capitulate in our war on drugs any more than we should surrender in our war on terrorism. Indeed, our ability to meet the long-term demands of the war on terrorism depends in part on our vigilance in combating drug trafficking and drug use among youth. The post-9-11 world demands clear thinking and moral resolve among adults and a commitment to teach that moral clarity to our children.

Back-pedaling on drug laws would be one of the worst examples we could give our children at this crucial moment in American history. On Nov. 5, voters in Arizona, Nevada, and Ohio should say no to the drug legalization movement's advance on their home fronts. None of us should embrace the call to legitimize more drug traffic. Our country, our communities, and our children deserve better.

1. All three ballot measures were defeated.

"*[Marijuana] arrestees are almost always peaceful, first-time offenders, but they are frequently housed with violent criminals.*"

Marijuana Prohibition Laws Unfairly Imprison Minor Offenders

Pete Brady

According to Pete Brady in the following viewpoint, the vast majority of marijuana arrests involve possession, not sale, of the drug. He believes harsh drug laws have filled American jails with nonviolent, first-time marijuana offenders. These minor offenders, he asserts, are often beaten and raped by their violent cellmates. Brady compares the conditions in U.S. jails to those at Abu Ghraib prison in Iraq, where American and British soldiers abused Iraqi prisoners. In American jails, he maintains, the abuse of marijuana offenders by other inmates is too often encouraged. Pete Brady is a writer and medical marijuana user.

As you read, consider the following questions:

1. According to Brady, why do a high percentage of people arrested for marijuana spend time in jails rather than prisons?
2. Why did the Arizona Court of Appeals award inmate Jeremy Flanders $635,000, in the author's contention?
3. Name four consequences of being arrested for marijuana, according to Brady.

Many people were shocked to see the photographs of American soldiers abusing Iraqi prisoners at Abu Ghraib [prison in Iraq]. Few Americans are aware that similar abuses take place every day in jails across the country. Marijuana prisoners and other non-violent offenders are often subject to similar violence and degradation.

Last year [2003], a 19-year-old college student in Gainesville, Florida, was sentenced to four weekends in jail after being found guilty of "providing marijuana."

The student was placed in a jail cell with 35-year-old Randolph Jackson, who was awaiting trial for allegedly raping a Gainesville woman.

Jackson was surprisingly popular with the jail's guards. Two guards were fired for giving lenient cellblock privileges to the accused rapist, and for bringing other inmates to Jackson's cell at his request. According to police reports, Jackson raped some of those inmates, while four guards looked the other way.

On the student's first Friday night behind bars, Jackson held a weapon to the 19-year-old marijuana provider's throat, and raped him.

The Abuse of Marijuana "Criminals"

The fallout from these rapes included the official "discovery" that non-violent marijuana "criminals" were often jailed in cells with violent felons. The sheriff in charge of the jail said overcrowding and guard shortages made it difficult to segregate harmless offenders from violent criminals.

Prisoner rape is so epidemic in America that last year President [George W.] Bush signed the largely symbolic Prison Rape Elimination Act. It was promoted by lobbyists like Tom Cahill, who was beaten and raped in a Texas prison in 1968 after being arrested for anti-war protesting.

Cahill's experience is emblematic of another problem: police like arresting people for non-violent free speech protests, and for victimless "crimes" involving marijuana. The arrestees are almost always peaceful, first-time offenders, but they are frequently housed with violent criminals.

A high percentage of people arrested for marijuana or civil disobedience spend time in jails rather than prisons. Many have not been found guilty of any crime; they're in jail because they can't afford to post bail, or due to delays in getting a court hearing. If they go to trial and are convicted, they're usually sentenced to jail rather than prison, because most marijuana possession sentences are under a year, and sentences under a year are served in jails.

Jailhouse Blues

Most American jails are poorly funded and dangerous. The Maguire Correctional Facility in Redwood City, California, is typical of US jails. It's supposed to house no more than 688 inmates; but it houses 978. Some inmates are crammed 15 to a room, with no toilets, windows, or water.

It can be worse. In Maricopa County, Arizona, Sheriff Joe Arpaio brags that he spends more per day to feed his police dogs than he does to feed the 8,000 prisoners under his control.

Arpaio houses 2,000 prisoners in tents in the desert. In the summer, temperatures soar to 120°F (49°C). Arpaio's jails have been the subject of lawsuits and federal investigations since the early 1990's. His guards have been found guilty of brutality.

He also set up the first all-women's chain gang in history. The female inmates work as county cemetery gravediggers in the desert sun, burying indigents and dead babies.

Arpaio also created an Internet "JailCam" that showed prisoners being strip-searched, shackled in "restraint chairs," and women using the toilet.

In Arpaio's jails, inmates work seven days a week, are fed only twice a day, and have to pay $10 if they need medical care. The sheriff bought a military tank to assist in drug busts—but investigators say gangs and drug dealers pervade his jails.

In 1996, an inmate named Jeremy Flanders was beaten nearly to death by gang members in Arpaio's tent city jail; the Arizona Court of Appeals recently upheld a jury's damage award that gave Flanders $635,000 of taxpayer's money to compensate him for the injuries, which the court found "could have been prevented" if Arpaio had not been "deliberately indifferent" to existence of violent gangs in his jails. . . .

As of June 2003, US federal and state prisons and jails

The War on Drugs and Prisoner Rape as a "Management Tool"

The war on drugs never, ever had anything to do with public health. From its beginning in 1968, it was [President] Richard Nixon's scheme to politically neutralize young men of color and the predominately white counterculture of which I am a long-time member. And like most wars, it's been about political and economic expedience. The war on drugs is a civil war against America's poor. As in any war, in the name of national security, civil rights are suspended and atrocities are committed. And since more than half of the men, women and children locked-up in America are confined for drug-related crimes (a majority of them non-violent and victimless crimes), they should be more correctly called "political prisoners.". . .

The appalling conditions behind bars are scarcely conceivable in free society. Statistics do not provide a clear picture of these conditions, but they can begin to establish a useful perspective. For instance: In 1995, each day, 83,000 adult male prisoners were raped in US correctional institutions, according to a report by Stephen Donaldson, of SPR [Stop Prisoner Rape]. Donaldson's statistics have yet to be challenged by the Bureau of Justice Statistics. In fact Donaldson's statistics may be so conservative, he may be off by half. . . .

Who is being raped behind bars? It's certainly not the big drug lords or the vicious thugs in for murder and assault. It's mostly the young, non-violent, first-offenders confined for a little too much pot and too poor to buy their freedom who fit the victim profile. The legislators and judges know all this. It's their job to know.

A few politicians have spoken out. In 1970, in the wake of prison insurrections in our country, we find these comments on record: "The appalling conditions and practices in many of our penal institutions can do more damage to a young person than his use of marijuana," said then New York State Representative Ed Koch before he became Mayor of New York City.

Tom Cahill, *Alternatives Magazine*, Summer 1999.

housed 2,078,670 people, at an annual cost of $57 billion.

The US incarcerates people at a rate six to 10 times higher than most other "democracies." The US incarceration rate of 715 imprisoned per 100,000 residents compares to rates of 114 for Australia, 116 for Canada, 95 for France and 96 for Germany.

Approximately half of the 2.1 million people in America's prisons and jails are behind bars due to drug laws. The high incarceration rate is fueled by a high arrest rate; just over 697,000 Americans were arrested for marijuana crimes in 2002, and 88% of those arrests were for possession. Since 1992, nearly seven million Americans have been arrested for marijuana.

What harms can happen to a person arrested for marijuana? At minimum, being busted involves a gun-toting authority figure oppressing a person who feels that use of the plant should not be a crime. Being arrested for pot involves being detained, interrogated, forced to provide identification, held against one's will. It involves fear of punishment. It involves entering the byzantine labyrinth of the criminal justice system, at the mercy of guards, violent prisoners, bail bondsmen, jurors, judges, and attorneys. It involves expenditure of money.

In some cases, arrest and consequences of arrest are much harsher than the minimum. The arresting officers might injure or kill the arrestee, either by mistake or deliberately. The arrestee's family, loved ones, or friends might be harmed physically and emotionally. Police or courts might take an arrestee's possessions or money. If convicted of a marijuana crime, a person can lose school funding, child custody, professional credentials, the right to vote, the ability to get a good job.

If a marijuana "criminal" is sentenced to jail or prison, the prisoner is subject to many dangerous external forces. Most marijuana prisoners are gentle people, unequipped to defend themselves against the hardships of arrest and incarceration. They are often raped and beaten. They are scarred for life.

"The likelihood of jails being swelled by thousands of unlucky college students who were the victims of a drug bust targeting the otherwise innocent is very small."

Marijuana Prohibition Laws Do Not Imprison Minor Offenders

Iain Murray

It is a myth that the government frequently sends casual marijuana users to prison, argues Iain Murray in the following viewpoint. Only a small percentage of federal prisoners are serving time for marijuana possession, he points out. Murray asserts that most marijuana offenders in prison had prior convictions, and many inmates who were charged with simple marijuana possession had committed other secondary crimes. Also, through plea bargains, he claims, criminals often have serious charges reduced to simple marijuana possession. Murray is a senior fellow at the Competitive Enterprise Institute, a public policy organization.

As you read, consider the following questions:
1. According to the author, what percentage of marijuana offenders do U.S. attorneys decline to prosecute?
2. What evidence does Murray use to support his claim that federal authorities are not "prosecuting thousands of people for simply possessing a joint or two"?
3. In the author's contention, who is a typical federal drug offender?

Iain Murray, "Just Because They Got High . . . ?" www.technopolitics.com, September 1, 2001. Copyright © 2001 by Iain Murray. Reproduced by permission.

It has become a commonplace [assertion] that the main reason America's prison population exploded during the past ten years is because law enforcement authorities have cracked down on simple drug use, sending anyone they find simply puffing on a marijuana joint to the Big House for years on end. At a time when the most requested song on radio is Afroman's "Because I got high," the question of whether we are being too hard on pot smokers is an appropriate one. The latest figures from the Justice Department, however, suggest that we are not.

Commenting on the release of those figures on federal drug offenders in 1999, Attorney General John Ashcroft said, "Federal law enforcement is targeted effectively at convicting major drug traffickers and punishing them with longer lock-ups in prison." The *Washington Post*, however, summed up the mood of many when it editorialized, "The data the department [of Justice] released show almost exactly the opposite: that the nation's tough drug sentencing regime is, to a great extent, being used to lock up comparatively low-level offenders who could easily be prosecuted in state courts."

At first glance, this reasoning seems correct: the figures show that 7,128 defendants were convicted of offenses involving marijuana as the most serious substance involved, which amounts to 31 percent of the total number convicted for drug offenses. Crack offenses provided only 22 percent, powder cocaine 21 percent and methamphetamine 12 percent of the total. Moreover, US attorneys declined to prosecute less than 10 percent of suspects involved with marijuana. Surely here is prima facie evidence that pot users are being targeted disproportionately to their effect on society.

The Real Story About Marijuana Offenders

However, as always with government figures, there is a more complicated story hidden further within the statistics. To begin with, the idea that the federal authorities are prosecuting thousands of people for simply possessing a joint or two is clearly a myth. Of the 38,000 suspects evaluated for prosecution by US attorneys in 1999, only about 470 were investigated for simple possession of marijuana—less than one percent of the total. Besides, about a third of those charged with simple possession were charged with other, secondary offenses.

Moreover, let us not forget that the one charge that federal agents were able to make stick to the great 30s crime lord, Al Capone, was tax evasion. Simply because the charge isn't serious, it doesn't mean that the person charged is an innocent abroad. Over half of those charged had prior convictions (ten percent 5 or more), over a third were convicted felons, and just under a third were actually under criminal justice supervision at the time of their arrest. If the authorities are able to remove an habitual criminal from the streets with a possession charge, that is probably a good thing.

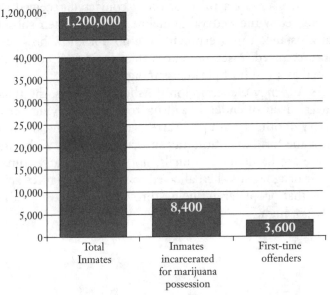

The Number of State Prison Inmates in Mid-2002 Who Were Incarcerated for Marijuana Possession

Created by book editor using statistics from the Office of National Drug Control Policy.

The same picture presents itself when prisoners in state and local jails are considered. About 27 percent of state prisoners are in jail for simple possession, and 13 percent are there for marijuana-related offenses. But a massive 82 percent of state prisoners have one or more prior convictions, and fully 54 percent were under some form of supervision at the time of their arrest. The likelihood of jails being swelled by thousands of unlucky college students who were the victims of a drug bust targeting the otherwise innocent is very small.

Plea Bargains Benefit Marijuana Criminals

A final factor that should be borne in mind is the plea bargain. Oftentimes, drug offenders will provide substantial assistance to the authorities in their inquiries in order to avoid the harsh mandatory sentences they would otherwise suffer. Having a charge involving crack reduced to a charge involving marijuana is a mutually beneficial result, not the massive misdirection of investigative effort some would have us believe. As if to bear this out, the Justice Department figures show that almost a third of those convicted received sentences below the Federal guideline range for their substantial assistance to government. We do not know how many more received lesser sentences than their true crime warranted as a result of plea bargaining.

As Attorney General [John] Ashcroft implies, the typical federal drug offender is a drug trafficker, preying on the misery of others, with prior arrests or convictions, often under some form of continuing supervision by the authorities. These are hardened criminals, not the innocent victims of unfair drug laws. When allowed to speak, the figures amply show that people aren't being thrown into jail just "because they got high."

"The war on drugs has become a war on suffering people."

Federal Laws Prohibiting the Use of Medical Marijuana Harm Patients

Christopher Largen

The federal government classifies marijuana as a harmful, addictive substance and forbids its use. However, some ill patients use the drug illegally to ease their nausea or pain. In the following viewpoint Christopher Largen, an author who has used marijuana therapeutically, maintains that the federal government denies patients access to a beneficial drug simply because some people abuse it. Prohibiting the use of medical marijuana for this reason is as ridiculous as banning junk food because some people are obese, he charges.

As you read, consider the following questions:

1. According to Largen, what was the main fear of the quadriplegic veteran who secretly used marijuana to ease his pain?
2. What facts does the author cite as proof that "marijuana is medicine"?
3. What two questions does Largen raise about the federal government's stance on medical marijuana?

The nightmare is always the same. I see [U.S. Attorney General] John Ashcroft standing behind a tall podium, hovering over me as his voice booms with the authority of a man with a satellite linkup to God. "In response to an obesity epidemic killing hundreds of thousands of Americans annually, our newly formed Food Enforcement Administration has outlawed junk food. Local police will conduct searches of residential refrigerators. Candy wrappers and barbeque grills are now considered paraphernalia. To dissuade the lucrative black-market activities of street gangs like the Ice Cream Crew and the Praline Posse, neighborhood weight-watch signs will be erected in your area. Pre-employment urine screenings will test for traces of illicit food substances. Fast food felons will no longer be allowed to vote, carry a handgun, or receive a Pell Grant. Our military forces will be dispatched to destroy African cocoa fields used in chocolate production. Police smuggling donuts will face corruption charges. And insulin-dependent diabetics will just have to suffer and die, because we don't want to send the wrong message to children about sugar abuse. Can you pinch more than an inch? If so, you aren't simply unhealthy, you're a criminal. So just say NO to Cracker Jacks!"

I wake up sweating, but then I take a deep breath, still happy to be walking down the green path. Come walk a mile in my shoes . . .

A Child's Use of Marijuana

I am the youngest therapeutic cannabis user on record in the United States. I smoked my first joint in 1971, when I was two years old.

I was a severely hyperactive toddler (even then, I was a hellion). When I bit my preschool teacher on the leg and smashed my fist through the living room window, my parents became desperate. Few people understood medical marijuana (or hyperactivity, for that matter) back then, but my parents had smoked for years. In fact, my father had graduated Magna Cum Laude from TCU [Texas Christian University], smoking every day, and was a communications professor at Drake [University] in Iowa—again, smoking daily.

My parents were Southerners. They knew folk remedies,

like rubbing sweet rum on the swollen gums of teething babies. They thought cannabis wouldn't harm me, and they suspected it might relax me. So they held the joint to my lips, telling me to suck it like a straw.

Mom and Dad were amazed by the results. The marijuana curbed my aggression, reduced my tantrums, elevated my mood, increased my appetite, and helped me sleep. My parents provided it to me for the next three years until I entered kindergarten. Then my doctor prescribed Ritalin, a then cutting-edge amphetamine with serious side effects. Ten years later, Ritalin would become one of the most over-prescribed substances in the nation. Parents enjoyed the sanitized convenience of behavior intervention in a pill, while their children often sold those same pills in the school playground.

Meeting Other Medical Marijuana Patients

In 1990 I had no idea I would become a professional writer. I was sweating my way through college. My mind was full, if not my stomach. I dined cerebrally devouring books and vegetarian gruel. Still, someone had to bring home the tofu.

I accepted a job as personal attendant for a quadriplegic veteran whose pain specialist secretly recommended marijuana for his agonizing and debilitating spasms. The unfortunate price of his relief was the terror of being thrown in jail. One night after smoking his medicine he asked me, "Do you really think they would take care of a guy like me if I was behind bars? Give me physical therapy? Wipe my ass? Would they know how to change out my catheter? I wouldn't even be able to defend myself. I could die in there."

While the veteran lived in fear, other patients were legally smoking marijuana grown and supplied by Uncle Sam. I met the fifth federal patient, George McMahon, when he first spoke at UNT [University of North Texas] in 1998. George receives 300 pre-rolled joints each month, to treat severe symptoms of pain, spasms, and nausea related to years of surgical and pharmaceutical maltreatment, repeated injuries, and a rare genetic condition called Nail Patella Syndrome, which can cause bone deformities, kidney failure, and immune system dysfunction. George and his wife Margaret were traveling the world speaking to legislators, police officials, educators, health care professionals, and patients about the medical value of cannabis.

Prior to being accepted to the government program in 1990, George had survived 19 major surgeries, took 17 pharmaceutical drugs daily, and depended on a wheelchair. For the past fourteen years, George has smoked ten government joints each day. During this time George hasn't had a single surgery or hospitalization, he no longer takes pharmaceuticals (aside from the occasional antibiotic), and he rides a bike. He is living proof that marijuana is medicine.

George was an inspiration. He could easily have been complacent, enjoying the benefits of consistent access to his medicine. Instead he was fighting for other patients. George told me that helping others gave him courage and strength to get up every morning. He struck me as a humble man with a strength that belied his illness.

A Potentially Dangerous Project

When I approached George about the prospects of writing a creative autobiography, neither of us had ever embarked on a project of this magnitude. Self-doubt would prove to be our first hurdle. George gazed at me skeptically while he smoked a government joint, speaking in a gravelly voice that reminded me of asphalt, ashtrays, and Iowa corn.

"You got what it takes to craft a silk purse out of a sow's ear?"

I smiled and said, "You aren't a sow's ear. Your story can change lives."

"It could be a long haul. You sure you're up to it?"

I paused to consider the potential ramifications of writing this book. I already had firsthand knowledge of the dangerous and unintended repercussions of speaking out. People had tried to hurt me on numerous occasions. I had once been physically assaulted by skinheads while protesting a Ku Klux Klan rally on the steps of the State Capitol in Austin, [Texas] on Martin Luther "Coon" day (as the KKK called it). My car had been repeatedly vandalized, once by fire. In response to my writings on drug policy reform, I'd received veiled, threatening letters from disturbed strangers. I knew how difficult it could be to have a rational dialogue with hysterical people, especially when the First Amendment is often treated like toilet paper.

I looked up at George and said, "I can take the heat."

George stared down as he put out his joint. "Let's do it."

Statement by George McMahon, Medical Marijuana Activist

Since March of 1990 I have been receiving a monthly prescription for medical marijuana from the federal government for my medical problems. I am one of only 34 known medically ill individuals who have been approved to use marijuana legally in the U.S. I suffer from a rare neurological disease known as Nail Patella Syndrome (NPS). There are only 200 known cases of this genetic disorder. Of those, eight percent are affected with organ and immune system complications, which kills most of them by the age of 40.

My sister died with NPS at age 44. My mother has NPS, but is only affected by slight joint deformities. When I was three, my father died at the age of 40 from a combination of tumors and tuberculosis. Today, in addition to fighting for my life, I am still [waging] a battle with marijuana.

Instead of legality for just a few others and myself, I am fighting to help scores of medically ill individuals who haven't received the privilege to use the drug legally. If one ill individual can legally use the drug and get some relief from their pain, I feel I have succeeded with my mission.

George McMahon, "Texas Patient George McMahon," Texans for Medical Marijuana.

We began with George pouring out a lifetime of memories into an old-school Dictaphone. Before we finished, the project blossomed into a major road trip documented on video, including stops at the State Capitol of Arkansas, Elvis Presley's Graceland, and the federal cannabis garden at Ole Miss [the University of Mississippi].

Over the past three years, I've had the honor of serving as George's co-author, caregiver, biographer, historian, devil's advocate, and publicity consultant. We've traveled through 11 states together, speaking at law schools, junior colleges, legislative gatherings, and music festivals. We've occasionally been followed, videotaped, and harassed by misguided police officers and attorney generals. But, we've also been welcomed by legislators, church librarians, and DEA [Drug Enforcement Administration] agents. And we've generated news articles in five countries with an aggregate circulation of approximately 20 million readers. Not bad for a couple of guys with no degrees, a couple of antiquated home computers, two very patient wives, several kamikaze editors, and a stubborn desire to dig ditches and help change the laws.

Medical Marijuana Patients Should Not Be Considered Criminals

The federal marijuana program lies at the heart of a conundrum that demands resolution. If the DEA is correct in claiming that marijuana is a dangerously addictive drug with no medical benefit, then why has the government been giving it to sick and dying people for the last 23 years? On the other hand, if marijuana has medical applications, why is the federal government criminalizing patients, closing clinics, and denying states the legal autonomy to resolve the issue independently? Until these questions are answered, George's story needs to be told, again and again.

Politics are intensely personal. Making no distinction between individual circumstances of use, the war on drugs has become a war on suffering people. Legislators aren't health care professionals, and patients aren't criminals. Yet health and law become entwined in a cruel and sometimes deadly dance.

After thirty years of perpetually escalating sentences and draconian prohibition policies, we've lost more of our citizens (and more of our civil liberties) than we did on September 11th [2001, when terrorists attacked America]. Despite this devastating human carnage, illegal drugs are still readily available on any given street corner in America. This is the terrible result of attempting to treat a public health problem as a criminal justice issue. It's like trying to outlaw junk food. It will never work.

How long will it take before our government implements drug policies that heal people rather than destroying lives? I'm no soothsayer, but I think we hold the answer in the voices we raise and the ballots we cast. Something tells me our journey down the green path has not yet ended.

Oh, yeah . . . and to all you fired-up activists, I'd like to offer some unsolicited knowledge (at the risk of sounding like [noted anthropologist] Margaret Mead). Never let yourself believe you can't make a difference. Indeed, you are the only one who can. And you don't have to be absorbed in some homogenized collective "movement" to change things, either. An organization is only as strong as its weakest link, but you are a majority of one. Act like it. Enough said.

"*Chronic, daily doses of [marijuana] . . . would unnecessarily expose the patients to [its] toxic effects.*"

Federal Laws Prohibiting the Use of Medical Marijuana Protect Patients

Eric A. Voth

Some states have passed laws that allow chronically ill patients to use marijuana medicinally. These laws are in violation of federal laws designed to shield people from potentially dangerous drugs. In the following viewpoint Eric A. Voth protests state ballot initiatives that allow patients to smoke medical marijuana and bypass the safety measures of the Food and Drug Administration. Marijuana is restricted, Voth argues, because it is addictive and harmful. Besides, he maintains, there is little evidence that marijuana safely and effectively treats pain, nausea, or other symptoms. Eric A. Voth is chairman of the Institute on Global Drug Policy and a clinical associate professor of medicine.

As you read, consider the following questions:
1. In Voth's view, what is significant about NORML, ACT, and the Cannabis Corporation of America?
2. According to the author, what are the problems with Lester Grinspoon's compilation of anecdotes that suggest marijuana has medicinal uses?
3. Name three dangers of marijuana, as cited by Voth.

Eric A. Voth, "A Peek into Pandora's Box: The Medical Excuse Marijuana Controversy," *Journal of Addictive Diseases*, vol. 22, December 11, 2003. Copyright © 2003 by The Haworth Press, Inc. Reproduced by permission.

The smoking of marijuana for medicinal applications is a volatile and difficult issue for the medical and regulatory communities. It has reached the forefront of discussions of public policy.

Any consideration of this issue must take into account the substantial toxicity, impurity, and morbidity associated with marijuana use. Several states have passed ballot initiatives or legislation that allow a medical excuse for possession of marijuana. These initiatives bypass the Food and Drug Administration process of proving safety and efficacy, and they have created serious regulatory dilemmas for state regulatory boards. Several examinations of the issue have consistently drawn question to the validity of smoking an impure substance while voicing concern for the well being of patients in need. . . .

The Classification of Marijuana

In 1972, the Department of Justice Drug Enforcement Administration (DEA) was petitioned to reschedule marijuana from a Schedule I drug (unable to be prescribed, high potential for abuse, not currently accepted for medicinal use, and lack of safety of the drug) to a Schedule II drug (high potential for abuse, currently accepted for [limited] medical use, but able to be prescribed).

This rescheduling petition was initiated by the National Organization for the Reform of Marijuana Laws (NORML), Alliance for Cannabis Therapeutics (ACT), and the Cannabis Corporation of America. It is significant that these organizations lobby for the legalization of marijuana and have neither a medical base, nor do they represent any accredited or respected medical entity.

Because of continued controversy surrounding the rescheduling of marijuana, Administrative Law Judge Francis Young was retained by the DEA in 1988 to rule on the merits of rescheduling marijuana to Schedule II. Judge Young ruled that marijuana should be rescheduled to Schedule II for nausea associated with cancer chemotherapy and [for] spasticity. He concluded, however, that insufficient evidence existed to warrant use of crude marijuana for glaucoma or other applications.

The administrator of the DEA ultimately denied the petition to reschedule. In the face of extensive expert testimony provided to the DEA which opposed the rescheduling of marijuana, the marijuana lobby only produced evidence consisting of anecdotes and testimony of a handful of physicians with limited or no clinical experience with the medical areas in question. During the rescheduling hearings it became clear that crude, especially smoked, marijuana had not been accepted as a medicine by any reputable medical entity.

The denial of the rescheduling petition by the DEA resulted in an appeal by marijuana advocates to the United States Court of Appeals for the District of Columbia. In a decision handed down in February 1994 the Court set forth the guidelines that only rigorous scientific proof can satisfy the requirement of "currently accepted medical use." Crude marijuana does not meet these guidelines.

Risky Medical Marijuana Initiatives

Several voter initiatives have been undertaken by marijuana advocates to circumvent the FDA process and the DEA scheduling rules. While not actually legalizing marijuana for medical use, the initiatives create a "defense to possession" for those possessing a medical recommendation to use marijuana. The ballot initiatives were heavily financed by individuals and organizations who seek the legalization of marijuana and other drugs. The funding bought media consultants, airtime, and legal expertise. While the initiatives were promoted as being "compassionate" for suffering patients, they also created legal protection to those claiming medical ailments as justification for possession and personal use.

The danger of such ballot initiatives is that they create an atmosphere of "medicine by popular vote" rather than the rigorous processes required by federal law that all medicines must undergo. There also exists great concern that the movement to accept marijuana for medicinal applications is having the secondary effect of softening public attitudes on marijuana use. In the 2002 election cycle, initiatives in Florida, Michigan, and Ohio ostensibly sought to require treatment for drug-related arrests. Underlying what would be perceived as a positive change, however, were no controls on what drugs nor what criminal acts would be eligible for treatment. Furthermore, the definitions of "treatment" were generally quite loose. Even literacy or vocational training could have qualified for hard core felons with long-standing drug problems. The Florida and Michigan propositions did not require drug abstinence even during treatment. All three created a situation where criminal addicts would have statutory preference for treatment over non-criminals and were deemed unconstitutional. . . .

Recently, the Justice Department filed an injunction in United States District Court against the Oakland Cannabis Buyers Cooperative [medical marijuana patients and providers] in an attempt to close down the apparent open dealing of marijuana. This injunction was overturned upon appeal. A subsequent appeal to the United States Supreme Court has set the legal tone for the medicinal marijuana issue. The Supreme Court ruled on May 14, 2001, that the Controlled Substances Act may not be violated by the sale of marijuana for medicinal purposes, and that there is no medical necessity exception to the Controlled Substances Act's prohibitions on manufacturing and distributing marijuana. The Supreme Court decision will likely have a chilling effect on future legislation and litigation regarding the use of marijuana for medicinal purposes.

Serious regulatory questions have also been raised regarding the standard of care that have not been adequately dealt with by ballot initiatives. These questions may serve as a template for regulatory boards who are faced with the medical excuse marijuana issue. Unfortunately, regulatory agencies have also been handed a difficult situation to assess. . . .

The Problems with Marijuana Research

In 1993, [doctor and marijuana advocate Lester] Grinspoon published a compilation of anecdotes which now serves as the bible of the "medical excuse marijuana" movement. He suggests that marijuana should be used for nausea associated with cancer chemotherapy, glaucoma, wasting in AIDS, depression, menstrual cramps, pain, and miscellaneous ailments. His anecdotes contained no controls, no standardization of dose, no quality control, and no independent medical evaluation for efficacy or toxicity.

The discussion of historical uses of marijuana cited in Grinspoon's book include such cultures as India, Asia, the Middle East, South Africa, and South America and are considered by the medical excuse marijuana movement as evidence of appropriate medical uses of the drug. The Chinese allegedly used marijuana to "quicken the mind, induce sleep, cure dysentery, stimulate appetite, relieve headaches, and cure venereal disease." One of Grinspoon's references from 1860 states marijuana provided beneficial medical effects "without interfering with the actions of the internal organs." Such folk medicine applications of marijuana from the 1700s and 1800s are referenced by the authors as evidence justifying the modern medical applications.

The field of medicine in those earlier years was fraught with potions and herbal remedies. Many of those were absolutely useless, or conversely were harmful to unsuspecting subjects. This situation gave rise to the development and evolution of our current Food and Drug Administration and drug scheduling processes.

Advocates of marijuana contend that the smoking of marijuana has the advantage of providing a rapidly absorbed . . . dose of THC [the active ingredient in marijuana]. While rapid absorption could be an advantage in some arenas, neither anecdotal nor controlled studies have delineated whether antiemetic [nausea-relieving] qualities appear before, after, or concurrent to the intoxicating effects. Indeed, the therapeutic end point for successful administration of smoked marijuana has not been established.

Smoked Marijuana Has Adverse Effects

Research on the utility of THC has demonstrated some effectiveness of the purified form of the drug in treating nausea associated with cancer chemotherapy or appetite stimulation, but even researchers are cautious about using smoked substances. [Researcher M.R.] Tramer [and associates] evaluated the state of the research on cannabinoids [chemicals in marijuana] and concluded that in selected patients they may be useful as mood enhancing agents, but serious adverse side effects will likely limit their usefulness. They also stated,

These results should make us think hard about the ethics of clinical trials of cannabinoids when safe and effective alternatives are known to exist and when efficacy of cannabinoids is known to be marginal. . . .

Several comprehensive reviews have been undertaken to assess the potential medical uses of marijuana. [Eric] Voth and [R.H.] Schwartz extensively reviewed available therapies for chemotherapy-associated nausea, glaucoma, multiple sclerosis, and appetite stimulation and concluded that no compelling need exists to make crude marijuana available as a medicine for physicians to prescribe. They recommended that the most appropriate direction for cannabinoid research is to research specific cannabinoids or synthetic analogs rather than pursuing the smoking of marijuana as a way to deliver THC.

Criteria for a Drug to Be Considered a Medicine

1. The drug's chemistry must be known and reproducible.
2. There must be adequate safety studies.
3. There must be adequate and well-controlled studies proving efficacy.
4. The drug must be accepted by *qualified* experts.
5. The scientific evidence must be widely available.

Eric A. Voth, "A Peek into Pandora's Box: The Medical Excuse Marijuana Controversy," *Journal of Addictive Diseases*, December 11, 2003.

Former Assistant Secretary of Health [Philip] Lee at the request of Congress solicited opinions from investigators at the National Institute on Allergy and Infectious Diseases, who commented on the AIDS wasting syndrome; the National Cancer Institute which commented on the use of marijuana as an antiemetic in cancer chemotherapy; the National Eye Institute which commented on marijuana's use in glaucoma; and the National Institute for Neurological Disorders and Stroke which commented on marijuana's role as an antispasticity drug in multiple sclerosis. The summary opinion stated:

This evaluation indicates that sound scientific studies supporting these claims are lacking despite anecdotal claims that smoked marijuana is beneficial. Scientists at the National Institutes of Health indicate that after carefully examining the existing preclinical and human data, there is no evidence to suggest that smoked marijuana might be superior to currently available therapies for glaucoma, weight loss associated with AIDS, nausea and vomiting associated with cancer chemotherapy, muscle spasticity associated with multiple sclerosis, or intractable pain.

The National Institutes of Health reconsidered this issue in 1997 and has called for further research into alternate delivery systems for pure THC as well as research into the comparative efficacy of marijuana with newer available medicines which have added heightened efficacy to medication regimes. The summary also expressed concern over pulmonary, neuro, and immunotoxicity of cannabis.

Marijuana Alternatives Should Be Researched

In 1997 the White House Office of National Drug Control Policy commissioned the National Academy of Science, Institute of Medicine (IOM) to evaluate the utility of marijuana for medicinal applications. The study concluded that the challenge for future research will be to find cannabinoids which enhance therapeutic benefits while minimizing side effects such as intoxication and dysphoria. Useful delivery systems for isolated or synthetic cannabinoids could include nasal sprays, metered dose inhalers, transdermal patches, and suppositories. The future for medicinal applications of cannabinoids and whether cannabinoids are equal or superior to existing medicines remains to be determined, but the IOM evaluation is particularly clear on the smoking of marijuana:

> If there is any future for marijuana as a medicine, it lies in its isolated components, the cannabinoids and their synthetic derivatives. Isolated cannabinoids will provide more reliable effects than crude plant mixtures. Therefore, the purpose of clinical trials of smoked marijuana would not be to develop marijuana as a licensed drug, but such trials could be a first step towards the development of rapid-onset, non-smoked cannabinoid delivery system.

The advocates for marijuana would have the public and policy makers incorrectly believe that crude marijuana is the only treatment alternative for large populations of patients who are inadequately treated for the nausea associated with chemotherapy, glaucoma, multiple sclerosis, and other ailments. Numerous effective medications are, however, currently available for conditions such as nausea. To date, no compelling data substantiates the existence of significant numbers of marginally treated or untreated patients for the maladies which marijuana is advanced.

Medical Complications of Marijuana Use

Marijuana continues to be widely used in our society. While its use declined in the late 1980s and early 1990s, a trend toward increasing use has recently been seen in high school students. Marijuana remains the most frequently used illegal drug. The chronic use of marijuana has now been demonstrated to be associated with higher utilization of the health care system and associated cost, a long suspected phenomenon.

The negative side effect profile of marijuana far exceeds most of the other effective agents available. In the studies performed to examine THC for chemotherapy-associated nausea, elderly patients could not tolerate the drug well. Chronic, daily doses of the drug would be necessary to treat many of the proposed medical conditions. This would unnecessarily expose the patients to the toxic effects.

Mental, affective, and behavioral effects are the most easily recognized consequences of acute and chronic marijuana use. Concentration, motor coordination, and memory are all adversely impacted.

The ability to perform complex tasks, such as flying [an aircraft], is impaired even 24 hours after the acute intoxication phase. The association of marijuana use with trauma and intoxicated motor vehicle operation is also well established. . . .

While the dependence-producing properties of marijuana are probably a minimal issue for chemotherapy-associated nausea when treatment is required short-term or sporadically, it is a major issue for the chronic daily use necessary for glaucoma, AIDS wasting syndrome, and other alleged chronic applications.

The respiratory difficulties associated with marijuana use preclude the inhaled route of administration as a medicine. Smoking marijuana is associated with higher concentrations of tar, carbon monoxide, and carcinogens than are found in cigarette smoking. Marijuana adversely impairs some aspects of lung function and causes abnormalities in the respiratory cell lines from large airways to the alveoli. Marijuana smoke causes inflammatory changes in the airways of young people that are similar to the effects of tobacco. In addition to these cellular abnormalities and consequences, contaminants of marijuana smoke are known to include various pathogenic bacteria and fungi. Those with impaired immunity are at particular risk for the development of disease and infection when these substances are inhaled.

*"After the Supreme Court's decision . . .
helping [sick] people could trigger federal
prosecution."*

The Federal Government
Should Not Override State
Medical Marijuana Laws

Sherry F. Colb

The federal government prohibits the use of marijuana for
any reason, yet numerous states have made it legal for patients with AIDS, cancer, and other chronic diseases to
smoke marijuana to relieve nausea and pain. On occasion the
federal government has overridden state laws and prosecuted medical marijuana users. In the following viewpoint
Sherry F. Colb, a Rutgers Law School professor, argues that
the federal government's interference with state laws legalizing medical marijuana is unfair. However, in 2005 the
Supreme Court ruled in *Raich v. Ashcroft* that the federal
government may continue to do so.

As you read, consider the following questions:
1. How does the author support her claim that Ed
   Rosenthal's actions did not contribute to the global drug
   trade or illegal trafficking?
2. Under what circumstances does legal regulation work as
   an instrument of social control, in Colb's contention?
3. In the author's opinion, what is one main difference
   between the fight of the segregationists and that of the
   medical marijuana growers?

Sherry F. Colb, "The Conviction of Ed Rosenthal for Growing Medicinal
Marijuana: Why It Was Wrong to Prosecute," *FindLaw*, February 12, 2003.
Copyright © 2003 by FindLaw, a Thomson business. This column originally
appeared on FindLaw.com. Reproduced by permission of the author.

[In January 2003], a federal jury in California convicted
Ed Rosenthal of marijuana cultivation and conspiracy
charges. Rosenthal will now face a minimum of five years
behind bars for his actions. Theoretically, he could even be
sentenced to life imprisonment.

People are convicted of drug offenses every day, of course.
But several factors distinguished this case from others.

First, Ed Rosenthal grew marijuana for sick and dying patients. Second, Rosenthal acted as an agent of Oakland, California's program to dispense marijuana to people whose
doctors have prescribed it. Third, California's Proposition
215 expressly authorized the program.[1]

At Rosenthal's trial, the defense sought to tell the jury
these facts, but the judge ruled them inadmissible. As a result, Rosenthal was convicted by a jury whose members believed he was an ordinary marijuana grower.

Following the verdict, upon learning the truth, several jurors called for a new trial. Horrified by what they had done,
they felt they had been misled into making a terrible mistake.

A Supreme Court Ruling

In a previous column, I argued that providing relief to suffering patients should qualify as a common law defense to
federal drug charges. In an opinion by Justice [Clarence]
Thomas in the case of *United States v. Oakland Cannabis Buyers Cooperative*, however, the U.S. Supreme Court rejected
such arguments.

In that case, a cooperative that dispensed marijuana to
sick people was seeking a declaratory judgment stating that
their activities were legal. Though they lost the case, no one
was sent to prison.

The decision, however, brought the war on drugs to a new
front. A battle that was once waged on unscrupulous dealers
would now come to those attempting to alleviate the agony
of extremely and terminally ill individuals.

Because marijuana can combat nausea, it is an invaluable
treatment for AIDS sufferers losing dangerous amounts of

---

1. As of June 2005 the federal government can prosecute medical marijuana users
even if they live in states that permit its use.

weight, and for cancer patients experiencing nausea induced by chemotherapy. After the Supreme Court's decision in *Oakland Cannabis Buyers Cooperative*, helping such people could trigger federal prosecution.

Warned that their activities violated federal law, California officials and citizens—including Ed Rosenthal—nonetheless persisted in doing what they thought was right. Perhaps they reasoned that even if federal narcotics laws technically prohibited what they were doing, they could count on the Justice Department to exercise its discretion wisely.

They might have hoped that, having made its point that the laws indeed apply, the Department would still use its resources to go after the kind of drug-dealing that can blight neighborhoods and go hand in hand with violence.

Rosenthal, after all, did not participate in the global drug trade, either by buying drugs of unknown origin from dealers or by selling them to the general population. Moreover, because his actions were regulated, like the actions of the alcohol industry after the end of Prohibition, they were not linked to the violence and mayhem of illegal drug trafficking.

In trusting federal prosecutors to leave them alone, however, Ed Rosenthal and others made a serious miscalculation.

Hypocrisy

Rather than look the other way, Attorney General [John] Ashcroft and his Justice Department have chosen to pursue Ed Rosenthal for openly flouting the dictates of federal law. Under the Constitution's Supremacy Clause, federal law trumps state law whenever the two conflict.

For the federal government to insist that all citizens in every state adhere to federal law is not inherently objectionable. Many states, for example, disagreed with the U.S. Supreme Court's view of segregation in *Brown v. Board of Ed.* Indeed, the phrase "state's rights" became a synonym for racism and segregation in part because states took the position that integration was a bad idea, regardless of how loudly a group of tyrannical federal judges insisted otherwise.

Most of us think, however, that when segregationists stood behind their beliefs with massive resistance, the federal government acted appropriately in crushing that resistance. It was doing what was necessary to ensure that African-American children could safely attend the same public schools as their white counterparts.

The merits of the underlying dispute are therefore an inescapable part of any condemnation of the Rosenthal prosecution.

The Jurors in the Ed Rosenthal Case Speak Out

There was another group of victims in [the Rosenthal] case, whose protests demonstrate what this trial is really about. They are the jurors, who were coerced into delivering the literally preordained guilty verdict on [January 31, 2003].

Now that they are safely beyond the vengeful reach of the federal leviathan they are speaking out and objecting to being used to give the color of justice to the proceedings. They were clearly coerced into the verdict, but now they are seeking to avoid being accomplices to this crime.

One juror was quoted as saying, "it seems like we made a horrible mistake." Another was in tears and said she was afraid that they would be arrested if they defied the judge and voted their consciences. Yet another said, "I feel used. It's horrible. We didn't get the whole picture."

The jury foreman said, "We were made to feel like we had no choice, even though we were residents of a state that has legalized medical marijuana." As far as the federal government is concerned, that is irrelevant. In fact, the term "medical marijuana" could not even be mentioned in the trial. . . .

Jurors were told by Judge [Charles] Breyer, "You cannot substitute your sense of justice, whatever that is, for your duty to follow the law." At least Breyer did not add "whatever that is" after the word "law," but that elision does not alter the fact that "justice" is not the issue, only federal power, whatever that is.

Richard Cowan, *Marijuana News*, February 3, 2003.

Attorney General Ashcroft is nonetheless an easy target. He heads the Justice Department of an Administration that claims to value the sovereignty of states as well as the states' ability to embrace priorities that are distinct from those of the national government. In fact, the man who selected Ashcroft would not be in office were it not for an electoral approach that subordinates the will of the majority of the populace to the will of a group that more closely approximates the wishes of the states.

When Ashcroft and the [George W.] Bush Administration do not like what the states are doing, however, then their skepticism about federal supremacy seems to undergo a transformation. If California believes in medical marijuana, then California must be beaten into submission. Even if one does not accept the notion of a state's "right," one can still point a finger at those who do and who nonetheless go ahead and violate that putative right.

There's only so far the hypocrisy point can take us, however. Just because Ashcroft may be a hypocrite does not make the prosecution of Ed Rosenthal wrong. At best, it deprives Ashcroft of the moral standing to pursue it, leaving open the question of what a more principled attorney general ought to have done.

The State Government Sanctioned Rosenthal's Actions

There is something very troubling about the prosecution of Rosenthal, above and beyond the merits of the argument for a medical marijuana exception to narcotics laws.

Consider a similar but fictional set of facts. Suppose that Compassionate Carl decides to grow marijuana for sick people in New Jersey because he believes that both federal and state laws are wrong.

Carl feels strongly about what he does, just like Ed Rosenthal did, but Carl has no official authorization for his mission. In pursuing his agenda, however just and right, he engages in civil disobedience with his eyes open. He is as likely as any other drug-dealer to be charged with a crime.

State or federal prosecutors could decide to go after Carl under such circumstances, because he chooses to disobey laws of which he disapproves. A person like Carl might be willing to disregard other laws as well, and such a person therefore poses a risk of general lawlessness. In addition, if Carl gets away with his crime, then others may infer that one need only obey laws of which one approves.

Legal regulation works as a communal instrument of social control only if it compels compliance independent of any individual's views.

The next civil disobedient to follow in Carl's footsteps, then, might choose a far less controversial set of prohibitions to violate, perhaps because he and others have developed contempt for law. There is thus something to be said for following the rules, even when a person is not a fan of a particular statute.

Ed Rosenthal, however, did not simply choose to disobey the law. State officials specifically granted him permission to cultivate marijuana. In other words, whatever civil disobedience occurred was joined by the government of the state and the municipality, which might thus have appeared prepared to shield the individual from the wrath of the federal government.

This Battle Is Similar to That of the Desegregationists

If we go back to the case of massive resistance to desegregation, we have another example of federal lawbreaking assisted by state officials. In spite of the states' involvement, however, most of us would not feel that the federal government was wrong to intervene. In fact, federal intervention became the only hope of children seeking equality in the classroom.

Does the analogy to segregationists' massive resistance make the official recognition of Ed Rosenthal in California irrelevant? No. It only proves that if people are fighting for racial segregation, then they are engaged in activities that are so clearly wrong that the fight is benighted, regardless of who joins in. The fight against racial integration reflected and reinforced white supremacy.

Unlike the segregationists, the state of California and the selected official medicinal marijuana-growers in that state are engaged in something whose worthiness of condemnation is far less clear. Even people who believe that illicit drugs exact a horrific physical and moral cost on their users, would not generally equate provision for medicinal with provision for recreational use.

In considering the Rosenthal conviction, then, a number

of factors turn out to be significant. First is the nature of the defendant's actions. Ed Rosenthal grew marijuana to relieve the suffering of sick people, and he harmed no one in the process. Second is the fact that he went to great lengths to ensure that his actions conformed to the law of California, by obtaining official authorization. And finally, the Administration that chose to prosecute Rosenthal was guilty, in so doing, of hypocrisy.

Because California is not alone in singling out the medical use of marijuana for protection, the Justice Department has apparently decided to make an example of Ed Rosenthal. He is dangerous because he dissents from the Attorney General's position.

Whether the issue is medicinal marijuana, our failure to execute enough people in the Northeast, or the legalization of physician-assisted suicide in Oregon, it seems, Ashcroft considers dissenters to be enemies of the State (or at least, of the federal government).

"Allowing traffickers to carry on with impunity . . . undercuts enforcement of the [federal] Controlled Substances Act."

The Federal Government Should Override State Medical Marijuana Laws

Laura M. Nagel

Although the use of marijuana is prohibited by federal law, some states have legalized the drug for medicinal use by patients with painful conditions such as cancer. In the following viewpoint, originally given as testimony before the House of Representatives on March 27, 2001, Laura M. Nagel asserts that state laws legalizing medical marijuana undermine the efforts of the Drug Enforcement Administration (DEA) to stop marijuana trafficking and run afoul of federal law. In 2005 the Supreme Court ruled that medical marijuana users can face federal charges regardless of whether the drug is legal in their state. Laura M. Nagel is deputy assistant administrator of the DEA's Office of Diversion Control.

As you read, consider the following questions:
1. How much medical marijuana is a person allowed to possess in Oakland, California, according to Nagel?
2. What are the stipulations of the international drug treaties that the United States must follow, according to the author?

Laura M. Nagel, statement before the U.S. House Subcommittee on Criminal Justice, Drug Policy, and Human Resources, Committee on Government Reform, Washington, DC, March 27, 2001.

The majority of controlled substances are in Schedules II through V.[1] Some drug substances were placed in Schedule I by Congress in 1970 and others added in subsequent years because of their high potential for abuse and lack of medical safety and use in the United States. These actions have withstood the test of time and scientific scrutiny and remain there today. These control actions have saved an indeterminable number of lives within the United States. However, the CSA [Controlled Substances Act] has proved to be a dynamic law that has allowed for the evolution of science and technology to progress to the point in which some Schedule I substances have been developed for medical use and the CSA has been modified from its original listings to bring new drug products to the general medical community.

State Medical Marijuana Laws Cause Conflict

I would now like to address the impact state laws such as California's Proposition 215 have had on federal law enforcement. These state laws purport to legalize marijuana for "medical" use. These so-called "medical marijuana laws" work as follows: If a doctor "recommends" that a patient use marijuana for any ailment, then it is legal for the patient to grow and use marijuana. At present, Alaska, California, Colorado, Hawaii, Maine, Nevada, Oregon, and Washington have passed such laws. Arizona has passed a law that allows doctors to prescribe any Schedule I drug. Contrary to these laws, marijuana remains an illegal drug under federal law.[2] Actually "medical" marijuana is actually a misnomer since marijuana is in fact a Schedule I drug. As such, it has not been scientifically proven safe and effective in accordance with the Food, Drug, and Cosmetic Act and cannot be used except in research approved by the FDA [Food and Drug Administration] and registered with DEA [Drug Enforcement Administration]. Under federal law, there is really no basis to distinguish "medical" marijuana trafficking from marijuana trafficking generally.

1. Substances with the potential for abuse are placed in one of five categories ranging from Schedule I, the most restrictive category, to Schedule V, the least restrictive.
2. The 2005 Supreme Court case *Raich v. Ashcroft* affirmed the federal government's right to indict any medical marijuana user.

Historically, DEA has directed its investigative resources at major trafficking organizations without regard to whether the traffickers might claim to have a "medical" excuse for violating the law. This is not to say that these current state laws have not caused conflict and confusion throughout the law enforcement community. California's Attorney General publicly announced his unwillingness to enforce the state's drug laws against traffickers who claim to be involved with "medical" marijuana. He has left it to the individual counties and municipalities to arrive at their own criteria for implementation of Proposition 215. The California localities that have taken a public position on Proposition 215 have issued vague guidelines, all of which send a clear message that anyone who has a "recommendation" from a doctor is permitted to grow and possess certain amounts of marijuana. The City of Oakland for example allows each person to possess up to six pounds of marijuana. Since there is a complete lack of state government oversight, each grower is on his or her honor not to exceed these vague guidelines.

California has now become the home of several "cannabis" clubs that openly distribute marijuana to anyone who the club owners decide has a "medical" need for the drug. In some jurisdictions, local sheriffs have given groups advance permission to grow marijuana while state judges have ordered law enforcement officials to return marijuana seized from criminal defendants who claim to be handling the drug for "medical" reasons. Even where local police have made arrests and seizures, there have been numerous instances where local district attorneys have been unwilling to prosecute because the defendants supposedly complied with the "spirit" of Proposition 215.

Marijuana Trafficking Under State Law

An example of how marijuana trafficking is occurring under the guise of medicine is illustrated in one particular case in 1999. A local television station in New Orleans informed law enforcement officials that it had discovered an Internet web site advertising the sale of "medical" marijuana. The web site was established by an individual who distributed marijuana from his home in Anaheim, California. After the United

States Attorney's Office for the Eastern District of Louisiana advised DEA that it would prosecute the case, DEA undercover agents placed orders which resulted in marijuana being shipped to the agents in New Orleans. In September 1999, agents from the DEA and IRS [Internal Revenue Service] together with the Anaheim Police Department executed a search warrant at the defendant's home. During the execution of the warrant, the defendant advised that he had been selling "medical" marijuana for nearly three years. Records revealed that he had distributed more than 50 pounds to 149 different customers in 35 different states. On February 11, 2000, the defendant was indicted by a federal grand jury in New Orleans on charges of distribution of marijuana and advertising the distribution of a Schedule I controlled substance. During the execution of the search warrant, agents also seized numerous "recommendation" letters that appear to have been issued by doctors in various states to customers.

State Medical Marijuana Laws Appear to Endorse the Drug

[There is a] profound correlation in benchmark surveys of drug use, which show that the more people who believe a drug is harmful, the fewer people use that drug. Equally profound are the surveys' findings that the reverse is also true: the fewer people who believe a drug is harmful, the more people use that drug. These surveys show that perception of harm with respect to marijuana has been dropping off annually since the renewal of the drive to legalize marijuana as medicine, which began in the early 1990s when legalization advocates first gained a significant increase in funding and began planning the state ballot initiative drive to legalize crude marijuana as medicine. The surveys are the Monitoring the Future Survey, which has tracked drug use among American high school students annually since 1975 and the National Household Survey on Drug Abuse, which has tracked drug use among Americans ages 12 and older annually or less frequently since 1972.

John D. Ashcroft et al. v. Angel McClary Raich et al., 03-1454, in the Supreme Court of the United States, 2004.

The resulting dilemma has been further viewed as jeopardizing the historical cooperation between federal, state, and local drug enforcement officials. For example, local officers assigned to a federally funded task force might find themselves in the situation of having to seize marijuana in order to enforce federal law, knowing that the local prosecutor will refuse to prosecute or the local judge will order the marijuana returned to the grower. In essence, allowing traffickers to carry on with impunity in this manner simply undercuts enforcement of the Controlled Substances Act and allows an unproven and potentially dangerous drug to be sold to the public as "medicine."

Two pending lawsuits have developed from law enforcement efforts to keep this situation in check. In *United States vs. Oakland Cannabis Buyers' Cooperative* the U.S. sought an injunction ordering this "cannabis club" to stop growing and distributing marijuana in violation of federal law. The club claimed a "medical necessity" defense that allowed it to distribute marijuana. The Ninth Circuit Court of Appeals recognized that this was a legally cognizable defense. The United States Supreme Court will hear argument on this case on March 28th, 2001.[3] In *Conant vs. ONDCP, DOJ, DEA, and HHS*[4] a group of Californians sued the Government claiming that doctors have a "free speech" right to "recommend" that their patients use marijuana in violation of federal law. The federal district court agreed and issued an injunction that prohibits DEA. from investigating doctors who "recommend" marijuana or revoking their DEA registrations.

State Medical Marijuana Laws Undermine International Treaties

Lastly, I would like to point out that the United States is a party to several international treaties to control international and domestic traffic in controlled substances. These are expressly recognized by Congress in the Controlled Substances Act. Most notable are: the 1961 Single Convention on Narcotic Drugs; the 1971 Convention on Psychotropic

---

3. It found that medical marijuana growers and distributors can be prosecuted under federal law.   4. The case was *Marcus Conant et al. v. John P. Walters, Director of the White House Office of National Drug Control Policy; Asa Hutchinson, Administrator, U.S. Drug Enforcement Administration; John Ashcroft, Attorney General of the United States; and Tommy G. Thompson, Secretary of the Department of Health and Human Services.*

Substances; and the 1988 Convention Against Illicit Traffic in Narcotic Drugs and Psychotropic Substances. Most of the provisions of the CSA must be in force in order for the United States to meet its obligations under these treaties. Treaty obligations that are relevant are as follows: the United States must enact and carry out legislation disallowing the use of Schedule I drugs outside of research; make it a criminal offense, subject to imprisonment, to traffic in illicit [drugs] or to aid and abet such trafficking; and prohibit cultivation of marijuana except by persons licensed by, and under the direct supervision of the federal government.

There is no doubt that Proposition 215 and similar state initiatives provide an obstacle to the United States meeting its obligations under these treaties. In addition, allowing these state marijuana initiatives to remain in force potentially undermines diplomatic efforts by the United States to persuade other countries like Mexico and Colombia to enact and vigorously enforce their drug laws.

Periodical Bibliography

The following articles have been selected to supplement the diverse views presented in this chapter.

Tom Cahill — "Torture in the American Gulag," *Alternatives Magazine*, Summer 1999.

Common Sense for Drug Policy — "Drug War Facts," March 1999. www.csdp.org.

Richard Cowan — "Why 'Drug' Testing Is Really Just Marijuana Testing—Which Is Counterproductive," January 20, 1998. www.marijuananews.com.

Deseret Morning News — "Mandatory Sentences Mean Minimum Justice," September 19, 2004.

Thelton Henderson, interviewed by PBS Frontline — *Busted: America's War on Marijuana*, Winter 1997–1998. www.pbs.org.

Asa Hutchinson et al., interviewed by Jeff Greenfield — "The War on Drugs," CNN's Greenfield at Large, July 17, 2001.

Gregory Kane — "Uneven Drug Sentencing Is Liberalism, Not Racism," *Sun (Baltimore)*, August 12, 2000.

Mark Kleiman, interviewed by PBS Frontline — *Busted: America's War on Marijuana*, Winter 1997–1998. www.pbs.org.

Marijuana Policy Project — "Update on Victims of the War on Medical Marijuana," *Marijuana Policy Report*, Spring 2004. www.mpp.org.

George McMahon — "Texas Patient George McMahon," Texans for Medical Marijuana. www.texansformedical marijuana.org.

Doug McVay — "An American Gulag in the Making; the Use of Mandatory Minimum Sentencing Laws Are Filling Our Prisons," *Orlando Sentinel*, September 29, 2002.

Debra Saunders — "West Takes on East in the Drug War," July 29, 2002. www.townhall.com.

U.S. Supreme Court — *John D. Ashcroft et al. v. Angel McClary Raich et al.*, 03-1454, www.supremecourtus.gov.

John P. Walters — "Just Say No . . . to Treatment Without Law Enforcement," *Weekly Standard*, March 6, 2001.

Should Marijuana Be Legalized?

Chapter Preface

In February 2003 Drug Enforcement Administration (DEA) agents, K-9 units, and postal inspectors raided the home and business of actor Tommy Chong, known for his role in the Cheech and Chong movies. His business, Chong Glass, sold pipes and water pipes that were allegedly designed for smoking cannabis. After confiscating the accessories and $120,000 in proceeds, the DEA stated that these products fit the law's definition of "drug paraphernalia": objects primarily intended for the use of illegal drugs. Chong and dozens of other individuals had been the focus of an investigation into the manufacture and sale of drug paraphernalia. As a result of the investigation, fifty-five pipe makers and sellers were indicted. For each count they faced three years in prison, a fine of $250,000, or both. Chong pled guilty to conspiring to sell marijuana paraphernalia online, was sentenced to nine months in prison, and was fined $20,000.

What makes this case significant is that authorities have generally concentrated their efforts on marijuana, not on paraphernalia used to smoke the drug. People who believe cannabis is harmful and should remain illegal think the sale of these products promotes drug use. They advocate prohibition of smoking accessories and the prosecution of people who sell them. Other commentators object, believing that paraphernalia should be permissible and that law enforcement resources would be better spent on charging drug dealers or combating what they see as more dangerous drugs. This conflict illustrates the differing views on the efficacy and fairness of marijuana laws.

Many argue that the government should prosecute anyone who sells marijuana paraphernalia. However, doing so is arduous. Usually the products have legitimate purposes; pipes and water pipes, for example, may be legally sold as tobacco pipes. Authorities and others concerned about the harms of marijuana contend that the current legal status of these products hampers efforts to curb drug use. They point out that pipe sales are illegal only if sellers *believe* the accessories will be used for illegitimate purposes, and proving what sellers know is difficult. Therefore, they maintain, the sale of these accessories for *any* purpose should be banned. They further oppose the sale of these products because they feel it sends the message that drug use is acceptable, safe, and even fun. "[Smoke] shops sell a dangerous lie and the equipment for addiction," asserts drug czar John Walters. DEA administrator John B. Brown adds, "People selling drug paraphernalia are in essence no different than drug dealers."

Some analysts, however, find fault in the prosecution of pipe makers and sellers. Carl Churchill, a former glass pipe artisan, argues that pipe makers are no more responsible for how their creations are used than are gun makers, who, he points out, are not held accountable for crimes committed using their products. He protests, "Tobacco pipe artisans cannot be held accountable for illegal drugs being smoked in their products! . . . Pipe makers cannot control their customer's intentions any more than gun makers can!" Often buyers do have good intentions, artisans claim; some people purchase glass pipes as display pieces. Members of the staff of It's All Goodz in Phoenix, Arizona, maintain that they create intricate, finely decorated pipes, water pipes, and other accessories as a form of self-expression. For example, the store's multicolored memorial piece, blown in honor of Derek Hoffman, who died a year after founding It's All Goodz, "is for display and remembrance, *not* for sale," stresses the staff. Prohibition of this glasswork, pipe makers contend, would violate free expression. Moreover, prosecuting pipe sellers, some people assert, does not decrease marijuana use.

Those who use pipes legitimately or who feel marijuana causes fewer problems than other drugs think law enforcement should not spend time indicting pipe sellers; most also contend that cannabis should be legalized and its trade regulated. On the other hand, many analysts argue that paraphernalia manufacturers should be put on trial, and that legalizing marijuana would ultimately harm society. The authors in the following chapter debate the harms and benefits of marijuana legalization. Whether law enforcement will continue to target the manufacturers and sellers of pipes remains to be seen.

> *"The government should treat marijuana*
> *. . . the same way it treats alcohol: It*
> *should regulate it, control it, tax it, and*
> *only make it illegal for children."*

Marijuana Should Be Legalized

Ethan A. Nadelmann

Many Americans support legalizing marijuana, claims Ethan
A. Nadelmann, founder and director of the Drug Policy Alliance. In the following viewpoint he asserts that the criminalization of marijuana is destructive and costly, much like
alcohol prohibition was in the 1920s. The war on marijuana
sends casual users to prison and costs taxpayers billions of
dollars, he claims. Cannabis legalization, on the other hand,
has been beneficial in the Netherlands, Nadelmann notes.
Since legalization, the use of marijuana has not increased in
that country and its sale has been effectively regulated, he
contends.

As you read, consider the following questions:
1. According to Nadelmann, how does marijuana
   legislation differ from other laws?
2. What question will arise from the increasing emergence
   of medical marijuana distributors, in Nadelmann's
   opinion?
3. In the author's contention, why did the commissioners of
   the Wickersham Report oppose repeal of the alcohol
   prohibition?

Ethan A. Nadelmann, "An End to Marijuana Prohibition: The Drive to Legalize
Picks Up," *National Review*, July 12, 2004, pp. 29–30. Copyright © 2004 by
National Review, Inc., 215 Lexington Ave., New York, NY 10016. Reproduced by
permission.

Never before have so many Americans supported decriminalizing and even legalizing marijuana. Seventy-two percent say that for simple marijuana possession, people should not be incarcerated but fined: the generally accepted definition of "decriminalization." Even more Americans support making marijuana legal for medical purposes. Support for broader legalization ranges between 25 and 42 percent, depending on how one asks the question? Two of every five Americans—according to a 2003 Zogby poll—say "the government should treat marijuana more or less the same way it treats alcohol. It should regulate it, control it, tax it, and only make it illegal for children."

Close to 100 million Americans—including more than half of those between the ages of 18 and 50—have tried marijuana at least once. Military and police recruiters often have no choice but to ignore past marijuana use by job seekers. The public apparently feels the same way about presidential and other political candidates. Al Gore, Bill Bradley, and John Kerry all say they smoked pot in days past. So did Bill Clinton, with his notorious caveat. George W. Bush won't deny he did. And ever more political, business, religious, intellectual, and other leaders plead guilty as well.

Marijuana Prohibition Is Costly, Foolish, and Destructive

The debate over ending marijuana prohibition simmers just below the surface of mainstream politics, crossing ideological and partisan boundaries. Marijuana is no longer the symbol of Sixties rebellion and Seventies permissiveness, and it's not just liberals and libertarians who say it should be legal, as [*National Review* writer] William F. Buckley Jr. has demonstrated better than anyone. As director of the country's leading drug policy reform organization, I've had countless conversations with police and prosecutors, judges and politicians, and hundreds of others who quietly agree that the criminalization of marijuana is costly, foolish, and destructive. What's most needed now is principled conservative leadership. Buckley has led the way, and New Mexico's former governor, Gary Johnson, spoke out courageously while in office. How about others?

Marijuana prohibition is unique among American criminal laws. No other law is both enforced so widely and harshly and yet deemed unnecessary by such a substantial portion of the populace.

Police make about 700,000 arrests per year for marijuana offenses. That's almost the same number as are arrested each year for cocaine, heroin, methamphetamine, Ecstasy, and all other illicit drugs combined. Roughly 600,000, or 87 percent, of marijuana arrests are for nothing more than possession of small amounts. Millions of Americans have never been arrested or convicted of any criminal offense except this. Enforcing marijuana laws costs an estimated $10–15 billion in direct costs alone. . . .

Effects of the Medical Marijuana Movement

The . . . battle, of course, concerns whether marijuana prohibition will ultimately go the way of alcohol Prohibition, replaced by a variety of state and local tax and regulatory policies with modest federal involvement. Dedicated prohibitionists see medical marijuana as the first step down a slippery slope to full legalization. The voters who approved [state] medical-marijuna ballot initiatives (as well as the wealthy men who helped fund the campaigns) were roughly divided between those who support broader legalization and those who don't, but united in seeing the criminalization and persecution of medical marijuana patients as the most distasteful aspect of the war on marijuana. (This was a point that Buckley made forcefully in his columns about the plight of [AIDS and cancer patient] Peter McWilliams, who likely died because federal authorities effectively forbade him to use marijuana as medicine.)

The medical marijuana effort has probably aided the broader anti-prohibitionist campaign in three ways. It helped transform the face of marijuana in the media, from the stereotypical rebel with long hair and tie-dyed shirt to an ordinary middle-aged American struggling with MS [multiple sclerosis] or cancer or AIDS. By winning first Proposition 215, the 1996 medical-marijuana ballot initiative in California, and then a string of similar victories in other states, the nascent drug policy reform movement demonstrated that it could win in the big leagues of American politics. And the emergence of successful models of medical marijuana control is likely to boost public confidence in the possibilities and virtue of regulating nonmedical use as well.

Looking at the Netherlands

In this regard, the history of Dutch policy on cannabis (i.e., marijuana and hashish) is instructive. The "coffee shop" model in the Netherlands, where retail (but not wholesale) sale of cannabis is *de facto* legal [legal by practice], was not legislated into existence. It evolved in fits and starts following the decriminalization of cannabis by Parliament in 1976, as consumers, growers, and entrepreneurs negotiated and collaborated with local police, prosecutors, and other authorities to find an acceptable middle-ground policy. "Coffee shops" now operate throughout the country, subject to local regulations. Troublesome shops are shut down, and most are well integrated into local city cultures. Cannabis is no more popular than in the U.S. and other Western countries, notwithstanding the effective absence of criminal sanctions and controls. Parallel developments are now underway in other countries.

Like the Dutch decriminalization law in 1976, California's Prop 215 in 1996 initiated a dialogue over how best to implement the new law. The variety of outlets that have emerged —ranging from pharmacy-like stores to medical "coffee shops" to hospices, all of which provide marijuana only to people with a patient ID card or doctor's recommendation—play a key role as the most public symbol and manifestation of this dialogue. More such outlets will likely pop up around the country as other states legalize marijuana for medical purposes and then seek ways to regulate distribution and access. And the question will inevitably arise: If the emerging system is successful in controlling production and distribution of marijuana for those with a medical need, can it not also expand to provide for those without medical need?

The Evolving Uses of "Medical" Marijuana

Millions of Americans use marijuana not just "for fun" but because they find it useful for many of the same reasons that

People Who Benefit from the War on Drugs Wish to Keep Marijuana Illegal

- I am a politician who has attracted a large constituency with my anti-drug rhetoric. I have gotten many anti-drug and rehab programs [funded] in my community. I can pontificate feel-good speeches and take the high moral ground with impunity. I generate very good-looking TV sound bites against the "War on Some Drugs".

- I am a member of a religion that teaches that only we are of high moral character and it is our duty and destiny to bring morality to the world, by whatever means necessary. Only we know what's best for everybody else.

- I am an agent in DEA/FBI/CIA/ABC/XXX and am allowed to seize "suspicious" money, cars, homes, airplanes, . . . or anything I think may have been involved with the drug trade. I can do it with impunity. The "War on Some Drugs" is a real power trip.

- I am a bank officer who has opened numerous accounts that deposit up to $9,999 in cash almost every day. 95% of that money I am legally allowed to loan or invest. . . .

- I am an employee of a jail/prison that did not exist until the quadrupling of incarcerations since 1980 because of the "War on Some Drugs".

- I am a bureaucrat who gets ten times the budget funding I ever got before the "War on Some Drugs" started.

- I am the owner of a drug rehabilitation facility that gets $20,000 a pop for a "client/patient" that has a successful "cure" rate of under 20%, which means I get about $100,000 to get a person off drugs. Most/all of the money comes [from] either insurance or government funding. It really doesn't cost you anything. . . .

- I am a career criminal with a history of violence. I am very glad the dope smokers have filled the jails and prisons because it means I always get out earlier because of "overcrowding".

Gösta H. Lovgren, "Why I Don't Want to Legalize Marijuana," Swede's Dock, www.exit109.com.

people drink alcohol or take pharmaceutical drugs. It's akin to the beer, glass of wine, or cocktail at the end of the workday, or the prescribed drug to alleviate depression or anxiety, or the sleeping pill, or the aid to sexual function and pleasure. More and more Americans are apt to describe some or all of their marijuana use as "medical" as the definition of that term evolves and broadens. Their anecdotal experiences are increasingly backed by new scientific research into marijuana's essential ingredients, the cannabinoids. Last year [2003], a subsidiary of *The Lancet*, Britain's leading medical journal, speculated whether marijuana might soon emerge as the "aspirin of the 21st century," providing a wide array of medical benefits at low cost to diverse populations.

Perhaps the expansion of the medical-control model provides the best answer—at least in the U.S.—to the question of how best to reduce the substantial costs and harms of marijuana prohibition without inviting significant increases in real drug abuse. It's analogous to the evolution of many pharmaceutical drugs from prescription to over-the-counter, but with stricter controls still in place. It's also an incrementalist approach to reform that can provide both the control and the reassurance that cautious politicians and voters desire.

The Failure of Prohibition

In 1931, with public support for alcohol Prohibition rapidly waning, President [Herbert] Hoover released the report of the Wickersham Commission. The report included a devastating critique of Prohibition's failures and costly consequences, but the commissioners, apparently fearful of getting out too far ahead of public opinion, opposed repeal. Franklin P. Adams of the *New York World* neatly summed up their findings:

> Prohibition is an awful flop.
>   We like it.
> It can't stop what it's meant to stop.
>   We like it.
> It's left a trail of graft and slime
> It don't prohibit worth a dime
> It's filled our land with vice and crime,
>   Nevertheless, we're for it.

Two years later, federal alcohol Prohibition was history.

What support there is for marijuana prohibition would likely end quickly absent the billions of dollars spent annually by federal and other governments to prop it up. All those anti-marijuana ads pretend to be about reducing drug abuse, but in fact their basic purpose is sustaining popular support for the war on marijuana. What's needed now are conservative politicians willing to say enough is enough: Tens of billions of taxpayer dollars down the drain each year. People losing their jobs, their property, and their freedom for nothing more than possessing a joint or growing a few marijuana plants. And all for what? To send a message? To keep pretending that we're protecting our children? Alcohol Prohibition made a lot more sense than marijuana prohibition does today—and it, too, was a disaster.

"It is time we adopted a marijuana policy that recognizes a distinction between use and abuse."

Marijuana Should Be Decriminalized

R. Keith Stroup

The following viewpoint is adapted from testimony given before the U.S. House of Representatives by R. Keith Stroup, who founded the National Organization for the Reform of Marijuana Laws. Because the prohibition of marijuana is destructive and wasteful, he contends, the drug should be decriminalized. Under a decriminalization model, Stroup explains, responsible cannabis use by adults would not be punishable by law. Removing marijuana penalties, he postulates, would end the arrest and imprisonment of thousands of productive and otherwise law-abiding citizens for drug use and possession. The government must allow individuals the freedom to choose to use cannabis responsibly, he concludes.

As you read, consider the following questions:

1. What are the three main points Stroup presents in support of his argument that marijuana should be decriminalized?
2. In the author's view, what was the underlying reason that law enforcement chose to investigate millionaire rancher Donald Scott?
3. According to Stroup, what four results stem from the government's "stubbornly defining all marijuana smoking as criminal"?

R. Keith Stroup, testimony before the U.S. House Subcommittee on Criminal Justice, Drug Policy, and Human Resources, Committee on Government Reform, Washington, DC, July 13, 1999.

The National Organization for the Reform of Marijuana Laws (NORML) has been a voice for nearly 30 years for Americans who oppose marijuana prohibition. A non-profit, public-interest lobby, NORML represents the interests of the millions of otherwise law-abiding citizens who smoke marijuana responsibly. [NORML advocates:]

(a) Complete decriminalization. NORML supports the removal of all penalties for the private possession and responsible use of marijuana by adults, cultivation for personal use, and the casual nonprofit transfers of small amounts. This model, generally called "decriminalization," greatly reduces the harm caused by marijuana prohibition by protecting millions of consumers from the threat of criminal arrest and jail. It represents a cease fire in the war against marijuana smokers; smokers would no longer be arrested, although commercial sellers would be.

(b) Regulation and legalization. NORML also supports the development of a legally controlled market for marijuana, where consumers could buy marijuana for personal use from a safe, legal source. This model is generally called "legalization." The black market in marijuana, and the attendant problems of crime and violence associated with an uncontrolled and unregulated black market, could be eliminated, as was the case when alcohol prohibition was ended in 1933, by providing consumers with an alternative legal market.

(c) Responsible use. Most importantly, marijuana smoking is not for kids and must be used responsibly by adults. As with alcohol consumption, it can never be an excuse for misconduct or other bad behavior. Driving or operating heavy equipment while impaired from marijuana should be prohibited. In addition, we recommend that responsible smokers adhere to emerging tobacco smoking protocols in public and private settings. The NORML Board of Directors has adopted the "Principles of Responsible Cannabis Use," available on our web site (www.norml.org), discussing acceptable conduct. . . .

Why Reform Is Needed

Current marijuana policy is a dismal and costly failure. It wastes untold billions of dollars in law enforcement resources, and needlessly wrecks the lives and careers of millions of our citizens. Yet marijuana remains the recreational drug of choice for millions of Americans.

Congress needs to move beyond the "reefer madness" phase of our marijuana policy, where elected officials attempt to frighten Americans into supporting the status quo by exaggerating marijuana's potential dangers. This is an issue about which most members of Congress are simply out of touch with their constituents, who know the difference between marijuana and more dangerous drugs, and who oppose spending $25,000 a year to jail an otherwise law-abiding marijuana smoker.

In fact, if marijuana smoking were dangerous, we would certainly know it; a significant segment of our population currently smokes marijuana recreationally, and there would be epidemiological evidence of harm among real people. No such evidence exists, despite millions of people who have smoked marijuana for years. So while we do need to fund more research on marijuana, especially research regarding medical uses—which, by the way, has been delayed by the federal government for years—we certainly know marijuana is relatively safe when used responsibly by adults.

It's time for Congress to let go of Reefer Madness, to end the crusade against marijuana and marijuana smokers, and to begin to deal with marijuana policy in a rational manner. The debate over marijuana policy in this Congress needs to be expanded beyond the current parameters to include consideration of (1) decriminalizing the marijuana smoker and (2) legalizing and regulating the sale of marijuana to eliminate the black market.

(a) Millions of mainstream Americans have smoked marijuana. It is time to put to rest the myth that smoking marijuana is a fringe or deviant activity engaged in only by those on the margins of American society. In reality, marijuana smoking is extremely common and marijuana is the recreational drug of choice for millions of mainstream, middle class Americans. Government's surveys indicate more than 70 million Americans have smoked marijuana at some point in their lives, and that 18–20 million have smoked during the last year. Marijuana is the third most popular recreational drug of choice for Americans, exceeded only by alcohol and tobacco in popularity.

A national survey of voters conducted by the American Civil Liberties Union (ACLU) found that 32%—one third of the voting adults in the country—acknowledged having smoked marijuana at some point in their lives. Many successful business and professional leaders, including many state and federal elected officials from both political parties, admit they used marijuana. It is time to reflect that reality in our state and federal legislation, and stop acting as if marijuana smokers are part of the crime problem. They are not, and it is absurd to continue spending limited law enforcement resources arresting them.

Increases in Severity of Marijuana Penalties Do Not Decrease Adolescent Usage Rates

Admitted use of marijuana by adolescents peaked in the late 1970s. A common assumption is that the intensified "drug war" of the 1980s caused the decline in usage rates. In fact, marijuana penalty increases (including lengthy mandatory minimum prison sentences) were not enacted until 1986. . . . Marijuana usage rates declined steadily at the same rate both before and after the penalty increase. Additionally, usage rates have increased during the 1990s, yet the harsher penalties have remained in place all the while.

In sum, just as removing or decreasing criminal penalties does not appear to increase marijuana use, adding or increasing penalties does not appear to decrease use.

Chuck Thomas, "Marijuana Prohibition Has Not Curtailed Marijuana Use by Adolescents," Marijuana Policy Project Foundation, December 1998.

Like most Americans, the vast majority of these millions of marijuana smokers are otherwise law-abiding citizens who work hard, raise families and contribute to their communities; they are indistinguishable from their non-smoking peers, except for their use of marijuana. They are not part of the crime problem and should not be treated like criminals. Arresting and jailing responsible marijuana smokers is a misapplication of the criminal sanction which undermines respect for the law in general.

Congress needs to acknowledge this constituency exists,

and stop legislating as if marijuana smokers were dangerous people who need to be locked up. Marijuana smokers are simply average Americans.

(b) Marijuana arrests have skyrocketed. Current enforcement policies seem focused on arresting marijuana smokers. The FBI reports that police arrested 695,000 Americans, the highest number ever recorded, on marijuana charges in 1997 (the latest year for which data are available), and more than 3.7 million Americans this decade; *83% of these arrests were for simple possession, not sale.* Presently one American is arrested on marijuana charges every 45 seconds. Approximately 44% of all drug arrests in this country are marijuana arrests. Despite criticism from some in Congress that President Bill Clinton was "soft" on drugs, annual data from the Federal Bureau of Investigation's (FBI's) Uniform Crime Report demonstrate that Clinton administration officials waged a more intensive war on marijuana smokers than any other presidency in history. Marijuana arrests more than doubled during President Clinton's time in office. This reality appears to conflict with statements by former White House Drug Czar Barry McCaffrey that America "cannot arrest our way out of the drug problem."

Unfortunately, this renewed focus on marijuana smokers represents a shift away from enforcement against more dangerous drugs such as cocaine and heroin. Specifically, marijuana arrests have more than doubled during the 1990s while the percentage of arrests for the sale of cocaine and heroin have fallen 51%. Drug arrests have increased 31% [since 1989], and the increase in marijuana arrests accounts for most of that increase.

(c) Marijuana penalties cause enormous harm. Marijuana penalties vary nationwide, but most levy a heavy financial and social impact for the hundreds of thousands of Americans who are arrested each year. In 42 states, possession of any amount of marijuana is punishable by incarceration and/or a significant fine. Many states also have laws automatically suspending the driver's license of an individual if they are convicted of any marijuana offense, even if the offense was not driving related.

Penalties for marijuana cultivation and/or sale also vary

from state to state. Ten states have maximum sentences of five years or less and eleven states have a maximum penalty of thirty years or more. Some states punish those who cultivate marijuana solely for personal use as severely as large-scale traffickers. For instance, medical marijuana user William Foster of Oklahoma was sentenced to 93 years in jail in January 1997 for growing 10 medium-sized marijuana plants and 56 clones (cuttings from another plant planted in soil) in a 25-square-foot underground shelter. Foster maintains that he grew marijuana to alleviate the pain of rheumatoid arthritis. Unfortunately, Foster's plight is not an isolated event; marijuana laws in six states permit marijuana importers and traffickers to be sentenced to life in jail.

Austere Marijuana Legislation

Federal laws prohibiting marijuana are also severe. Under federal law, possessing one marijuana cigarette or less is punishable by a fine of up to $10,000 and one year in prison, the same penalty as for possessing small amounts of heroin and cocaine. In one extreme case, attorney Edward Czuprynski of Michigan served 14 months in federal prison for possession of 1.6 grams of marijuana before a panel of federal appellate judges reviewed his case and demanded his immediate release. Cultivation of 100 marijuana plants or more carries a mandatory prison term of five years. Large-scale marijuana cultivators and traffickers may be sentenced to death.

Federal laws also deny entitlements to marijuana smokers. Under legislation signed into law in 1996 states may deny cash aid (e.g., welfare, etc.) and food stamps to anyone convicted of felony drug charges. For marijuana smokers, this includes most convictions for cultivation and sale, even for small amounts and nonprofit transfers. More recently, Congress passed amendments in 1998 to the Higher Education Act which deny federal financial aid to any student with any drug conviction, even for a single marijuana cigarette. No other class of offense, including violent offenses, predatory offenses or alcohol-related offenses, carries automatic denial of federal financial aid eligibility. While substance abuse among our young people is a cause for concern, closing the doors of our colleges and universities, making it more difficult for at-risk young people to succeed, is not an appropriate response to a college student with a minor marijuana conviction.

Even those who avoid incarceration are subject to an array of punishments that may include submitting to random drug tests, probation, paying for mandatory drug counseling, loss of an occupational license, expensive legal fees, lost wages due to absence from work, loss of child custody, loss of federal benefits, and removal from public housing. In some states, police will notify the employer of people who are arrested, which frequently results in the loss of employment.

In addition, under both state and federal law, mere investigation for a marijuana offense can result in the forfeiture of property, including cash, cars, boats, land, business equipment, and houses. The owner does not have to be found guilty or even formally charged with any crime for the seizure to occur; 80% of those whose property is seized are never charged with a crime. Law enforcement can target suspected marijuana offenders for the purpose of seizing their property, sometimes with tragic results. For example, millionaire rancher Donald Scott was shot and killed by law enforcement officials in 1992 at his Malibu estate in a botched raid. Law enforcement failed to find any marijuana plants growing on his property and later conceded that their primary motivation for investigating Scott was to eventually seize his land.

State and federal marijuana laws also have a disparate racial impact on ethnic minorities. While blacks and Hispanics make up only 20 percent of the marijuana smokers in the U.S., they comprised 58 percent of the marijuana offenders sentenced under federal law in 1995. State arrest and incarceration rates paint a similar portrait. For example, in Illinois, 57 percent of those sent to prison for marijuana in 1995 were black or Hispanic. In California, 49 percent of those arrested for marijuana offenses in 1994 were black or Hispanic. And in New York state, 71 percent of those arrested for misdemeanor marijuana charges in 1995 were nonwhite.

Prohibition Laws Are More Dangerous than Marijuana Itself

Arresting and jailing otherwise law-abiding citizens who smoke marijuana is a wasteful and incredibly destructive policy. It wastes valuable law enforcement resources that should be focused on violent and serious crime; it invites government into areas of our private lives that are inappropriate; and it frequently destroys the lives, careers and families of genuinely good citizens. It is time to end marijuana prohibition.

In 1972, a blue-ribbon panel of experts appointed by President Richard Nixon and led by former Pennsylvania Governor Raymond Shafer concluded that marijuana prohibition posed significantly greater harm to the user than the use of marijuana itself. The National Commission on Marijuana and Drug Abuse recommended that state and federal laws be changed to remove criminal penalties for possession of marijuana for personal use and for the casual distribution of small amounts of marijuana. The report served as the basis for decriminalization bills adopted legislatively in 11 states during the 1970s.

A number of other prestigious governmental commissions have examined this issue over the last 25 years, and virtually all have reached the same conclusion: the purported dangers of marijuana smoking have been greatly overblown and the private use of marijuana by adults should not be a criminal matter. What former President Jimmy Carter said in a message to Congress in 1977, citing a key finding of the Marijuana Commission, is equally true today: "Penalties against drug use should not be more damaging to an individual than the use of the drug itself. Nowhere is this more clear than in the laws against possession of marijuana in private for personal use."

The Decriminalization Model Is Popular and Effective

(a) Favorable experience with decriminalization in the U.S. Led by Oregon in 1973, 11 states adopted policies during the 1970s that removed criminal penalties for minor marijuana possession offenses and substituted a small civil fine enforced with a citation instead of an arrest. Today, approximately 30% of the population of this country live under some type of marijuana decriminalization law, and their experience has been favorable. The only U.S. federal study ever to compare marijuana use patterns among decriminal-

ized states and those that have not found, "Decriminalization has had virtually no effect on either marijuana use or on related attitudes about marijuana use among young people." Dozens of privately commissioned follow-up studies from the U.S. and abroad confirm this fact.

Decriminalization laws are popular with the voters, as evidenced by a 1998 state-wide vote in Oregon in which Oregonians voted 2 to 1 to reject a proposal, earlier adopted by their legislature, that would have reimposed criminal penalties for marijuana smokers. Oregonians clearly wanted to retain the decriminalization law that had worked well for nearly 30 years.

Since the Shafer Commission reported their findings to Congress in 1972 advocating marijuana decriminalization, over ten million Americans have been arrested on marijuana charges. Marijuana prohibition is a failed public policy that is out of touch with today's social reality and inflicts devastating harm on millions of citizens.

It is time we adopted a marijuana policy that recognizes a distinction between use and abuse, and reflects the importance most Americans place on the right of the individual to be free from the overreaching power of government. Most would agree that the government has no business knowing what books we read, the subject of our telephone conversations, or how we conduct ourselves in the bedroom. Similarly, whether one smokes marijuana or drinks alcohol to relax is simply not an appropriate area of concern for the government.

By stubbornly defining all marijuana smoking as criminal, including that which involves adults smoking in the privacy of their home, government is wasting police and prosecutorial resources, clogging courts, filling costly and scarce jail and prison space, and needlessly wrecking the lives and careers of genuinely good citizens.

It is time that Congress acknowledges what millions of Americans know to be true: there is nothing wrong with the responsible use of marijuana by adults and it should be of no interest or concern to the government.

In the final analysis, this debate is only incidentally about marijuana; it is really about personal freedom.

> "*Under legalization, which would decrease the cost [of marijuana] . . . and eliminate the legal risk, it is certain that the number of users would increase.*"

Marijuana Should Remain Illegal

John P. Walters

In the following viewpoint John P. Walters, director of the Office of National Drug Control Policy, argues that legalization of marijuana would have far more drawbacks than benefits. He contends that marijuana legalization would lead to increased use, especially among youths. According to Walters, marijuana causes the most social harm of any illegal drug, and advocates of marijuana legalization want to promote the use of all dangerous drugs.

As you read, consider the following questions:

1. In Walters's contention, how will legalization of marijuana make the task of law enforcement more difficult?
2. Name three examples cited by the author to support his assertion that the legalization movement ignores the benefits of marijuana prohibition.
3. How does the author respond to claims that youths will smoke less marijuana if it is high in potency?

John P. Walters, "No Surrender: The Drug War Saves Lives," *National Review*, vol. 56, September 14, 2004, p. 41. Copyright © 2004 by National Review, Inc., 215 Lexington Ave., New York, NY 10016. Reproduced by permission.

The prospect of a drug-control policy that includes regulated legalization has enticed intelligent commentators for years, no doubt because it offers, on the surface, a simple solution to a complex problem. Reasoned debate about the real consequences usually dampens enthusiasm, leaving many erstwhile proponents feeling mugged by reality; not so Ethan Nadelmann, whose version of marijuana legalization ("An End to Marijuana Prohibition," NR [*National Review*], July 12 [2004]) fronts for a worldwide political movement, funded by billionaire George Soros, to embed the use of all drugs as acceptable policy. Unfortunately for Nadelmann, his is not a serious argument. Nor is it attached to the facts.

To take but one example, Nadelmann's article alleges the therapeutic value of smoked marijuana by claiming: "Marijuana's medical efficacy is no longer in serious dispute." But he never substantiates this sweeping claim. In fact, smoked marijuana, a Schedule I controlled substance (Schedule I is the government's most restrictive category), has no medical value and a high risk of abuse. The Food and Drug Administration [FDA] notes that marijuana has not been approved for any indication, that scientific studies do not support claims of marijuana's usefulness as a medication, and that there is a lack of accepted safety standards for the use of smoked marijuana.

Drug Use Will Increase

The FDA has also expressed concern that marijuana use may worsen the condition of those for whom it is prescribed. Legalization advocates such as Nadelmann simply ignore these facts and continue their promotion, the outcome of which will undermine drug-prevention and treatment efforts, and put genuinely sick patients at risk. The legalization scheme is also unworkable. A government-sanctioned program to produce, distribute, and tax an addictive intoxicant creates more problems than it solves. First, drug use would increase. No student of supply-and-demand curves can doubt that marijuana would become cheaper, more readily available, and more widespread than it currently is when all legal risk is removed and demand is increased by marketing.

Second, legalization will not eliminate marijuana use among

young people any more than legalizing alcohol eliminated underage drinking. If you think we can tax marijuana to where it costs more than the average teenager can afford, think again. Marijuana is a plant that can be readily grown by anyone. If law enforcement is unable to distinguish "legal" marijuana from illegal, growing marijuana at home becomes a low-cost (and low-risk) way to supply your neighborhood and friends. "Official marijuana" will not drive out the black market, nor will it eliminate the need for tough law enforcement. It will only make the task more difficult. In debating legalization, the burden is to consider the costs and benefits both of keeping strict control over dangerous substances and of making them more accessible.

The Soros position consistently overstates the benefits of legalizing marijuana and understates the risks. At the same time, drug promoters ignore the current benefits of criminalization while dramatically overstating the costs. Government-sanctioned marijuana would be a bonanza for trial lawyers (the government may wake up to find that it has a liability for the stoned trucker who plows into a school bus). Health-care and employment-benefits costs will increase (there is plenty of evidence that drug-using employees are less productive, and less healthy), while more marijuana use will further burden our education system.

Marijuana Is Dangerous and Addictive

The truth is, there are laws against marijuana because marijuana is harmful. With every year that passes, medical research discovers greater dangers from smoking it, from links to serious mental illness to the risk of cancer, and even dangers from in utero exposure. In fact, given the new levels of potency and the sheer prevalence of marijuana (the number of users contrasted with the number of those using cocaine or heroin), a case can be made that marijuana does the most social harm of any illegal drug. Marijuana is currently the leading cause of treatment need: Nearly two-thirds of those who meet the psychiatric criteria for needing substance-abuse treatment do so because of marijuana use. For youth, the harmful effects of marijuana use now exceed those of all other drugs combined.

Remarkably, over 40 percent of youths who are current marijuana smokers meet the criteria for abuse or dependency. In several states, marijuana smoking exceeds tobacco smoking among young people, while marijuana has become more important than alcohol as a factor in treatment for teenagers. Legalizers assert that the justice system arrests 700,000 marijuana users a year, suggesting that an oppressive system is persecuting the innocent. This charge is a fraud. Less than 1 percent of those in prison for drug violations are low-level marijuana offenders, and many of these have "pled down" to the marijuana violation in the face of other crimes.

Legalization of Marijuana Endangers the Public

The vast majority of those in prison on drug convictions are true criminals involved in drug trafficking, repeat offenses, or violent crime. The value of legal control is that it enables judicial discretion over offenders, diverting minor offenders who need it into treatment while retaining the authority to guard against the violent and incorrigible. Further, where the sanction and supervision of a court are present, the likelihood of recovery is greatly increased. Removing legal sanction endangers the public and fails to help the offender. Proponents of legalization argue that because approximately half of the referrals for treatment are from the criminal-justice system, it is the law and not marijuana that is the problem.

Yet nearly half of all referrals for alcohol treatment likewise derive from judicial intervention, and nobody argues that drunk drivers do not really have a substance-abuse problem, or that it is the courts that are creating the perception of alcoholism. Marijuana's role in emergency-room cases has tripled in the past decade. Yet no judge is sending people to emergency rooms. They are there because of the dangers of the drug, which have greatly increased because of soaring potency. Legalization advocates suggest that youth will reduce their smoking because of this new potency. But when tobacco companies were accused of deliberately "spiking" their product with nicotine, no one saw this as a public-health gesture intended to reduce cigarette consumption.

The deliberate effort to increase marijuana potency (and market it to younger initiates) should be seen for what it is—

a steeply increased threat of addiction. Proponents of legalization argue that the fact that 100 million Americans admit on surveys that they have tried marijuana in their lifetime demonstrates the public's acceptance of the drug. But the pertinent number tells a different story. There are approximately 15 million Americans, mostly young people, who report using marijuana on a monthly basis.

Legalizing Marijuana Would Be Harmful

The wrong conclusion is that we have not made enough progress [in the war on drugs] and therefore we should legalize more harmful drugs. . . . There are three basic arguments legalizers present in saying we ought to change our policy. One: that the drug war is a failure. Two: that legalization would eliminate the profits and put the cartels out of business. Three: that drug use would decline. As to the myth that there has been no progress: There has been progress when we concentrate [fighting drug use] as a nation. . . .

The second main argument is that legalizing drugs will take the profit motive out of drugs and crime will go down. But you would have to legalize everything to take the criminal element out. Are the cartels going to be out of business if you legalize marijuana? I think they would also look at the heroin, cocaine and methamphetamine trade. . . . Law enforcement will always be necessary to protect our borders from organized crime and illegal drugs. . . .

Third, it is important that we learn from history. A legalized environment does not discourage drug use. We've engaged in this anti-drug effort not for 20 years as many people believe, but for 120 years. . . . Clearly, drug abuse is a historic problem in our country. We have fought this fight before. We have tried legalization and learned that it brings increased addictions and social costs.

Asa Hutchinson, "Let's Don't Punt on the Third Down," speech before the Commonwealth Club, February 12, 2002. www.commonwealthclub.org.

That is, only about 6 percent of the population age twelve and over use marijuana on a regular basis. To grasp the impact of legal control, contrast that figure with the number of current alcohol users (approximately 120 million). Regular alcohol use is eight times that of marijuana, and a large part of the difference is a function of laws against marijuana use. Under legalization, which would decrease the cost (now a little-noticed impediment to the young) and eliminate the legal risk, it is certain that the number of users would increase.

Hidden Motives of the Drug Legalization Movement

Can anyone seriously argue that American democracy would be strengthened by more marijuana smoking? The law itself is our safeguard, and it works. Far from being a hopeless battle, the drug-control tide is turning against marijuana. We have witnessed an 11 percent reduction in youth marijuana use over the last two years, while perceptions of risk have soared. Make no mistake about what is going on here: Drug legalization is a worldwide movement, the goal of which is to make drug consumption—including heroin, cocaine, and methamphetamine—an acceptable practice. Using the discourse of rights without responsibilities, the effort strives to establish an entitlement to addictive substances.

The impact will be devastating. Drug legalizers will not be satisfied with a limited distribution of medical marijuana, nor will they stop at legal marijuana for sale in convenience stores. Their goal is clearly identifiable: tolerated addiction. It is a travesty to suggest, as Ethan Nadelmann has done, that it is consistent with conservative principles to abandon those who could be treated for their addiction, to create a situation in which government both condones and is the agent of drug distribution, and to place in the hands of the state the power to grant or not grant access to an addictive substance. This is not a conservative vision. But it is the goal of George Soros.

> "*Marijuana, in its natural form, is one of the safest therapeutically active substances known.*"

Medical Marijuana Should Be Legalized

Marijuana Policy Project

According to the Marijuana Policy Project (MPP) in the viewpoint that follows, marijuana could help ease the suffering of millions of Americans if it were legalized. Although cannabis can safely relieve the symptoms of many ailments, the organization asserts, the U.S. government refuses to recognize its medical potential and continues to classify it as an addictive, dangerous drug. MPP, which educates Americans about marijuana legislation and lobbies to decriminalize marijuana, maintains that the majority of Americans supports legalizing cannabis for medicinal purposes.

As you read, consider the following questions:

1. How can marijuana benefit multiple sclerosis patients, in the MPP's contention?
2. In the author's opinion, what two discoveries resulted from the surge in recreational marijuana use in the 1970s?
3. According to the MPP, what were the findings of the CNN/*Time* poll published in 2002?

For thousands of years, marijuana has been used to treat a wide variety of ailments. Until 1937, marijuana (*Cannabis sativa L.*) was legal in the United States for all purposes. Presently, federal law allows only seven Americans to use marijuana as a medicine.

On March 17, 1999, the National Academy of Sciences' Institute of Medicine (IOM) concluded that "there are some limited circumstances in which we recommend smoking marijuana for medical uses." The IOM report, the result of two years of research that was funded by the White House drug policy office, analyzed all existing data on marijuana's therapeutic uses. Please see http://www.mpp.org/science.html.

Marijuana is one of the safest therapeutically active substances known. No one has ever died from an overdose, and it has a wide variety of therapeutic applications, including:

- Relief from nausea and appetite loss;
- Reduction of intraocular (within the eye) pressure;
- Reduction of muscle spasms; and
- Relief from chronic pain.

Marijuana is frequently beneficial in the treatment of the following conditions:

- *AIDS*. Marijuana can reduce the nausea, vomiting, and loss of appetite caused by the ailment itself and by various AIDS medications.
- *Glaucoma*. Marijuana can reduce intraocular pressure, alleviating the pain and slowing—and sometimes stopping—damage to the eyes. (Glaucoma is the leading cause of blindness in the United States. It damages vision by increasing eye pressure over time.)
- *Cancer*. Marijuana can stimulate the appetite and alleviate nausea and vomiting, which are common side effects of chemotherapy treatment.
- *Multiple Sclerosis*. Marijuana can limit the muscle pain and spasticity caused by the disease, as well as relieving tremor and unsteadiness of gait. (Multiple sclerosis is the leading cause of neurological disability among young and middle-aged adults in the United States.)
- *Epilepsy*. Marijuana can prevent epileptic seizures in some patients.
- *Chronic Pain*. Marijuana can alleviate the chronic, often

debilitating pain caused by myriad disorders and injuries.

Each of these applications has been deemed legitimate by at least one court, legislature, and/or government agency in the United States.

Many patients also report that marijuana is useful for treating arthritis, migraine, menstrual cramps, alcohol and opiate addiction, and depression and other debilitating mood disorders.

Marijuana could be helpful for millions of patients in the United States. Nevertheless, other than for the seven people with special permission from the federal government, medical marijuana remains illegal under federal law!

People currently suffering from any of the conditions mentioned above, for whom the legal medical options have proven unsafe or ineffective, have two options:

1. Continue to suffer without effective treatment; or
2. Illegally obtain marijuana—and risk suffering consequences directly related to its illegality, such as:
   - an insufficient supply due to the prohibition-inflated price or scarcity;
   - impure, contaminated, or chemically adulterated marijuana;
   - arrest, fines, court costs, property forfeiture, incarceration, probation, and criminal records.

Marijuana Prohibition

Prior to 1937, at least 27 medicines containing marijuana were legally available in the United States. Many were made by well-known pharmaceutical firms that still exist today, such as Squibb (now Bristol-Myers Squibb) and Eli Lilly. The Marijuana Tax Act of 1937 federally prohibited marijuana. Dr. William C. Woodward of the American Medical Association opposed the Act, testifying that prohibition would ultimately prevent the medicinal uses of marijuana.

The Controlled Substances Act of 1970 placed all illicit and prescription drugs into five "schedules" (categories). *Marijuana was placed in Schedule I, defining it as having a high potential for abuse, no currently accepted medical use in treatment in the United States, and a lack of accepted safety for use under medical supervision.*

This definition simply does not apply to marijuana. Of course, at the time of the Controlled Substances Act, marijuana had been prohibited for more than three decades. Its medicinal uses forgotten, marijuana was considered a dangerous and addictive narcotic.

A substantial increase in the number of recreational users in the 1970s contributed to the rediscovery of marijuana's medicinal uses:

• Many scientists studied the health effects of marijuana and inadvertently discovered marijuana's medicinal uses in the process.

• Many who used marijuana recreationally also suffered from diseases for which marijuana is beneficial. By accident, they discovered its therapeutic value.

As the word spread, more and more patients started self-medicating with marijuana. However, marijuana's Schedule I status bars doctors from prescribing it and severely curtails research.

In 1972, a petition was submitted to the Bureau of Narcotics and Dangerous Drugs—now the Drug Enforcement Administration (DEA)—to reschedule marijuana to make it available by prescription.

After 16 years of court battles, the DEA's chief administrative law judge, Francis L. Young, ruled:

> "Marijuana, in its natural form, is one of the safest therapeutically active substances known. . . .
>
> ". . . The provisions of the [Controlled Substances] Act permit and require the transfer of marijuana from Schedule I to Schedule II.
>
> "It would be unreasonable, arbitrary and capricious for DEA to continue to stand between those sufferers and the benefits of this substance. . . ."
>
> (September 6, 1988)

Marijuana's placement in Schedule II would enable doctors to prescribe it to their patients. But top DEA bureaucrats rejected Judge Young's ruling and refused to reschedule marijuana. Two appeals later, petitioners experienced their first defeat in the 22-year-old lawsuit. On February 18, 1994, the U.S. Court of Appeals (D.C. Circuit) ruled that the DEA is allowed to reject its judge's ruling and set its own criteria—enabling the DEA to keep marijuana in Schedule I.

However, Congress has the power to reschedule marijuana via legislation, regardless of the DEA's wishes.

Temporary Compassion

In 1975, Robert Randall, who suffered from glaucoma, was arrested for cultivating his own marijuana. He won his case by using the "medical necessity defense," forcing the government to find a way to provide him with his medicine. As a result, the Investigational New Drug (IND) compassionate access program was established, enabling some patients to receive marijuana from the government.

Luckovich. © 1999 by *Atlanta Constitution*. Reproduced by permission of Mike Luckovich and Creators Syndicate, Inc.

The program was grossly inadequate at helping the potentially millions of people who need medical marijuana. Many patients would never consider the idea that an illegal drug might be their best medicine, and most who were fortunate enough to discover marijuana's medicinal value did not discover the IND program. Those who did often could not find doctors willing to take on the program's arduous, bureaucratic requirements.

In 1992, in response to a flood of new applications from AIDS patients, the George H.W. Bush administration closed the program to new applicants, and pleas to reopen it were ignored by subsequent administrations. The IND program remains in operation only for the seven surviving, previously-approved patients.

Support for Legalizing Medical Marijuana Is Strong

There is wide support for ending the prohibition of medical marijuana among both the public and the medical community:

• Since 1996, a majority of voters in Alaska, California, Colorado, the District of Columbia, Maine, Montana, Nevada, Oregon, and Washington state have voted in favor of ballot initiatives to remove criminal penalties for seriously ill people who grow or possess medical marijuana. Polls have shown that public approval of these laws has increased since they went into effect.

• A CNN/*Time* poll published November 4, 2002, found that 80% of Americans believe that "adults should be allowed to legally use marijuana for medical purposes if their doctor prescribes it. . . ." Over the last decade, polls have consistently shown between 60% and 80% support for legal access to medical marijuana. Both a statewide Alabama poll commissioned by the *Mobile Register*, published in July 2004, and a November 2004 Scripps Howard Texas poll reported 75% support.

• Organizations supporting some form of physician-supervised access to medical marijuana include the American Academy of Family Physicians, American Nurses Association, American Public Health Association, the *New England Journal of Medicine*, and many others.

• A 1990 scientific survey of oncologists (cancer specialists) found that 54% of those with an opinion favored the controlled medical availability of marijuana and 44% had already suggested at least once that a patient obtain marijuana illegally.

"*The DEA is working . . . to make sure that those who need access to safe, effective pain medication can get the best medication available.*"

Safe and Effective Alternatives to Medical Marijuana Exist

Drug Enforcement Administration

Chronically ill patients are sometimes prescribed cannabis to ease their suffering. The Drug Enforcement Administration (DEA) insists in the following viewpoint that marijuana should not be used in this way because effective, federally approved alternative medicines are available. The agency asserts that a drug called Marinol delivers marijuana's active ingredient in a safe way. Because Marinol is taken orally, not smoked, it can relieve symptoms without exposing patients to harmful chemicals in smoke, the DEA contends. The DEA is the government agency that enforces America's controlled substances laws and works to reduce the availability of illegal drugs everywhere.

As you read, consider the following questions:
1. Name two problems with medical marijuana, as cited by the DEA.
2. What point does the author make about morphine?
3. According to the DEA, what were the recommendations of the Institute of Medicine's 1999 report?

Drug Enforcement Administration, "'Medical' Marijuana: The Facts," www.dea.gov.

"Medical" Marijuana: The Facts

- Medical marijuana already exists. It's called Marinol.
- A pharmaceutical product, Marinol, is widely available through prescription. It comes in the form of a pill and is also being studied by researchers for suitability via other delivery methods, such as an inhaler or patch. The active ingredient of Marinol is synthetic THC [the active ingredient in marijuana], which has been found to relieve the nausea and vomiting associated with chemotherapy for cancer patients and to assist with loss of appetite with AIDS patients.

Oversight by the Food and Drug Administration

- Unlike smoked marijuana—which contains more than 400 different chemicals, including most of the hazardous chemicals found in tobacco smoke—Marinol has been studied and approved by the medical community and the Food and Drug Administration (FDA), the nation's watchdog over unsafe and harmful food and drug products. Since the passage of the 1906 Pure Food and Drug Act, any drug that is marketed in the United States must undergo rigorous scientific testing. The approval process mandated by this act ensures that claims of safety and therapeutic value are supported by clinical evidence and keeps unsafe, ineffective and dangerous drugs off the market.
- There are no FDA-approved medications that are smoked. For one thing, smoking is generally a poor way to deliver medicine. It is difficult to administer safe, regulated dosages of medicines in smoked form. Secondly, the harmful chemicals and carcinogens that are byproducts of smoking create entirely new health problems. There are four times the level of tar in a marijuana cigarette, for example, than in a tobacco cigarette.
- Morphine, for example, has proven to be a medically valuable drug, but the FDA does not endorse the smoking of opium or heroin. Instead, scientists have extracted active ingredients from opium, which are sold as pharmaceutical products like morphine, codeine, hydrocodone or oxycodone. In a similar vein, the FDA has not

Marijuana Is Not Medicine

An issue of some note in California is the use of marijuana as medicine. Please understand that the DEA will not go out of business regardless of the directions Congress and the courts give us on this subject. Congress has designated marijuana as having no medicinal value. The Supreme Court affirmed this designation. The DEA must simply follow the law. What science has told us thus far is that there is no medical benefit from smoking marijuana; it is not recommended for treatment of any disease. It is appropriate for a doctor to prescribe Marinol, which has the active ingredient of marijuana. That can be taken in different forms, but the scientific community has not given conclusive results in regard to any benefit derived from smoking marijuana.

Asa Hutchinson, "Let's Don't Punt on the Third Down," speech before the Commonwealth Club, February 12, 2002. www.commonwealthclub.org.

approved smoking marijuana for medicinal purposes, but has approved the active ingredient—THC—in the form of scientifically regulated Marinol.

Research on THC's Usefulness

- The DEA [Drug Enforcement Administration] helped facilitate the research on Marinol. The National Cancer Institute approached the DEA in the early 1980s regarding their study of THC in relieving nausea and vomiting. As a result, the DEA facilitated the registration and provided regulatory support and guidance for the study.
- The DEA recognizes the importance of listening to science. That's why the DEA has registered seven research initiatives to continue researching the effects of smoked marijuana as medicine. For example, under one program established by the state of California, researchers are studying the potential use of marijuana and its ingredients on conditions such as multiple sclerosis and pain. At this time, however, neither the medical community nor the scientific community has found sufficient data to conclude that smoked marijuana is the best approach to dealing with these important medical issues.
- The most comprehensive, scientifically rigorous review of studies of smoked marijuana was conducted by the

Institute of Medicine, an organization chartered by the National Academy of Sciences. In a report released in 1999, the Institute did not recommend the use of smoked marijuana, but did conclude that active ingredients in marijuana could be isolated and developed into a variety of pharmaceuticals, such as Marinol.

- In the meantime, the DEA is working with pain management groups, such as Last Acts, to make sure that those who need access to safe, effective pain medication can get the best medication available.

Periodical Bibliography

The following articles have been selected to supplement the diverse views presented in this chapter.

Andrea Barthwell — "A Haze of Misinformation Clouds Issue of Medical Marijuana," *Los Angeles Times*, July 23, 2003.

Nancy Bellingham — "Is Mary Jane Really Bad?" *Canadian Speeches*, July 2001.

Brandeis University — "Recent Ballot Measures Indicate Need to Legalize Marijuana," *America's Intelligence Wire*, November 12, 2002.

Community Anti-Drug Coalition of America — "'Medical' Marijuana." www.cadca.org.

Cynthia Cotts — "Marijuana Made Easy," *Nation*, September 20, 1999.

Drug Enforcement Administration — "Speaking Out Against Drug Legalization." www.dea.gov.

Jerry Estes — "Drug Legalization and the Rest of the Story," County of Santa Barbara District Attorney, 2002. www.countyofsb.org.

Lancet — "Deglamorising Cannabis," November 11, 1995.

Marijuana Policy Project — "Medical Marijuana Briefing Paper," 2003. www.mpp.org.

Robert Mathias — "Novel Cannabinoid Appears Promising for Treatment of Chronic Pain," *NIDA Notes*, July 2004. www.nida.nih.gov.

Jenny Messmer — "High Times Rising"? *B-Cause*, Indiana University, Bloomington, Spring 2004. www.journalism.indiana.edu.

Ethan A. Nadelmann — "The Future of an Illusion: On the Drug War Believe Your Own Eyes," *National Review*, September 14, 2004.

Amanda L. Stevens — "Legalizing Marijuana Allows Police to Focus on Violent Crimes," *Raw Story*. www.rawstory.com.

Jacob Sullum — "Ernest Money," *Reason*, February 20, 2004.

John P. Walters — "Marijuana Today: Setting the Record Straight," *SF Gate*, September 1, 2002.

CHAPTER 4

What Should Be Done to Limit Marijuana Use?

Chapter Preface

In the fall of 2003, lawmakers voted to continue subsidizing a youth antidrug media campaign costing $150 million per year. With the funds the campaign produces antimarijuana messages that appear on television, billboards, subways, and bus shelters to inform youths that marijuana is dangerous. Additionally, many of the advertisements advocate for the war on drugs and claim that legalization of marijuana would be disastrous. To counteract those messages drug policy reform groups asked public transit authorities to post their notices proclaiming that cannabis is harmless and should be legalized. The authorities agreed. The resulting display of what some call "pro-marijuana" advertisements on public transit has upset many people who feel that the signage sends mixed signals to youths and undermines efforts to curb marijuana use. On the other side of the debate are those who believe they have a right to protest the government's tough stance on marijuana. They do not think publicizing their opinions encourages drug use. The debate over marijuana signage illustrates how contentious efforts to reduce marijuana use have proven to be.

Offended by antidrug war messages posted by Washington's metro system, Congressman Ernest Istook took action. He, like many politicians, is dedicated to reducing his country's drug use, believing that "saying 'no' to drugs is saying 'yes' to . . . a safer and more secure America." He was surprised and dismayed that the public transit system had posted signs calling for cannabis legalization and was even more shocked that some had provided the advertising space at no cost to drug policy reform groups. Istook asserted, "We provide major funding to combat drug use, and tax dollars should not be used to subsidize contrary messages." In protest he authored legislation to prohibit messages critical of drug laws from being posted by mass transit systems that receive federal funds.

Under Istook's amendment public transportation systems that disregarded the ban would lose federal funds ranging from almost $100,000 up to $3.1 billion. In a radio interview the congressman said of marijuana policy reformers, "They can use different means of advertising if they want to. They don't have to use a public property." Voicing a deeper concern about children's exposure to the messages, he added, "[Drug reform groups] do not have to use a bus that in Washington, DC, is used not only for general public's transportation but is also used as a school bus." In June 2004, however, Istook's amendment was struck down by Judge Paul Friedman as unconstitutional because it presented only one view of marijuana laws. The congressman indicated that the case was far from over: "I'm confident that ultimately the courts will agree with the long-standing principle that Congress is free to decide what we will or will not fund."

While many people agree that youths should not use marijuana, some complain that placing pro-drug war advertisements in public venues while banning messages that question cannabis legislation constitutes viewpoint discrimination, which is illegal. Moreover, many analysts refute Istook's claim that drug policy reform groups want Congress to fund their messages. Steve Fox of the Marijuana Policy Project declares, "Congress has given the White House Office of National Drug Control Policy hundreds of millions of taxpayer dollars to convey this message, but now that advocates of marijuana policy reform want to promote an alternative viewpoint—with their own money, no less—marijuana prohibitionists in Congress are trying to silence them." Siding with the drug policy reform groups, Judge Friedman wrote, "Just as Congress could not permit advertisements calling for the recall of a sitting Mayor or Governor while prohibiting advertisements supporting retention, it cannot prohibit advertisements supporting legalization of a controlled substance while permitting those that support tougher drug sentences."

While critics of the failed legislation believe it violated their right to avow that marijuana is not as dangerous as the government claims, supporters of Istook's amendment continue to feel that pro-marijuana legalization messages are confusing to youths and undercut efforts to combat marijuana use. In the following chapter authors argue over the best ways to reduce marijuana use in America, whether through antimarijuana campaigns, treatment for marijuana abusers, or government suppression programs.

"With marijuana, we want to teach [kids]
the facts. We want it to be their decision
... to never use."

D.A.R.E. Prevents Marijuana Use

Brett Richardson and Leann Richardson

For its *Busted: America's War on Marijuana* series, PBS Frontline conducted an interview with two full-time D.A.R.E. officers, Brett and Leann Richardson. The following viewpoint was excerpted from that interview. In it the Richardsons claim that the publicly funded Drug Abuse Resistance Education program that many schoolchildren participate in effectively dissuades them from using marijuana. Through D.A.R.E., the Richardsons assert, officers can reduce demand for marijuana by teaching children about its dangers. They also deny allegations that D.A.R.E. officers encourage kids to turn in family members who use marijuana.

As you read, consider the following questions:
1. What is a sore subject for D.A.R.E. officers, according to Leann Richardson?
2. In Brett Richardson's contention, what effect does drug use have on society?
3. What three facts has Brett Richardson learned about marijuana that help him better educate kids about its dangers?

Interviewer: How much of your time as a police officer is now taken up with D.A.R.E. [Drug Abuse Resistance Education]?

Brett Richardson: I'm a full-time D.A.R.E. instructor, so during the school year my sole responsibility is being at one of my schools. I have five schools—that means I'm at one school every day of the week, 8–4. The chief that we have, currently, is very supportive of the D.A.R.E. program, believes in it and that's why we have three full-time instructors.

How big is the force? How many officers do you have?

Brett Richardson: Thirty-five sworn officers and three of them are D.A.R.E. officers.

Are all three of you full-time with D.A.R.E.?

Brett Richardson: Yes. Two of us do the elementary schools and then Leann does the two middle schools and high school level.

D.A.R.E.'s Goal Is Prevention, Not Surveillance

There are some people who would say that you sort of are encouraging kids to spy on their family, parents. What's your answer to them?

Brett Richardson: No, we don't encourage the kids to spy. I don't care. I don't want to know. If they don't want to tell me, I don't want to know. That's not my role. I'm there as an instructor, not as an enforcement officer. I would just as soon not know about who's doing the marijuana in the home. I'm there for the child. I'm another resource.

I want to be a positive role model. I'm drug-free. I tell them that. I don't use alcohol, I don't use tobacco, I don't use any illegal substance. Two weeks ago, we did random drug testing at the police department, second time now my name's come up. I walked in here at the police station, the chief walked past me, said, "Brett, go out to MedStat, your name came up." So I went out, did my drug test. I tell the kids that was fine with me, I didn't have anything to hide. I'm there as an instructor. I'm not there to gather information. I don't encourage the kids to tell. It's by their choice if they want to come to me and tell me, "Mom or dad's using drugs, what do I do?" or "I'm really scared because my dad smokes." Those are the kind of issues we deal with.

Leann Richardson: I think that's a sore subject with us, especially with the D.A.R.E. program, because we don't go in and teach these kids, "This is how to do surveillance on your parents," or "This is what we want you to look for." It's not that type of a curriculum. It's a prevention curriculum that we go in and we teach these kids life skills, we teach them how to be safe, we teach them how to live a healthy lifestyle, drug-free. And it has nothing in the curriculum about turning people in or doing anything that way.

If a child, for some reason, feels uncomfortable about the home environment, about something that's happening in their life, that's where we are and in our relationship with them, as one more person for these kids to come over and talk to, not as an undercover officer, or even as a police officer. We go in there without a gun belt, as a human resource for these kids, as someone who really cares about these kids.

Reducing Demand Through Education

You're trying to create a kind of non-drug culture to compete with the drug culture.

Brett Richardson: We want to encourage them to not use drugs, because of the health effects, and then the effects it has on society. Taxpayers are upset with all the taxes we're paying. It doesn't make me happy as a taxpayer to hire more police officers, build bigger jails, build more courts, hire more judges—that costs me money. So if we can reduce overall criminality, not only drugs, but reduce vandalism, reduce theft, shoplifting, all those issues, then we're helping society. And as a police officer I see that as my role. I'm here to help people and to reduce crime.

But you're trying to paint a picture of marijuana that competes with another picture that you'd be getting from peer pressure.

Leann Richardson: With marijuana, we want to teach them the facts. We want it to be their decision, and their choice to never use. We believe if they know the facts about drugs, whether it's marijuana, tobacco, alcohol, or any other drugs, if they know the facts, they can make a logical choice for their own lives. And that's what we're wanting to do.

Do you think it's possible, though, to create a non-drug culture, especially with something like marijuana. Do you think you can create a world where there's no marijuana use?

Leann Richardson: The only way we're going to work on the war against drugs, or win the war on drugs, is to reduce the demand. And we're trying to reduce the demand through education, and that's why we got involved in the D.A.R.E. program. We wanted to be a part of the kids' lives, to help them to make good choices and learn how to resist peer pressure.

Realistic Goals

Brett Richardson: They warned me, when I went to the Illinois State Police Academy for my D.A.R.E. training, that you're going to go into that classroom with the belief that you'll save all those children. That all of your D.A.R.E. students will always remain 100% drug-free, and for the first years that's the way I felt. I wanted all of my students, every one of those children, to never use drugs.

In Defense of D.A.R.E.

Apple pie, motherhood, baseball and DARE—quite frankly—all deserve defending. . . . No course would be more morally, physically and spiritually destructive to America's next generation than choosing drug legalization over common-sense, fact-based education, such as that promoted by . . . DARE. . . .

While the 18-to-25 age cohort (no longer in contact with fact-laden DARE officers, dedicated teachers and parents) has suffered a 28 percent increase in current use between 1997 and 1999, youth users of marijuana fell by 2.3 million between 1997 and 1998. . . . According to [drug czar] Barry McCaffrey, this "remarkable success" is due, in no small measure, to "the DARE program."

Bobby Charles, *Washington Times*, September 10, 2000.

Nine years later, I'm a little more realistic in my thinking. But my desire is still for every one of my D.A.R.E. students to be 100% drug-free. The reason I feel that way is because I know what drugs do to the body. Through my education of learning about the drugs, learning about marijuana, what effects it has on the human body, what it's going to do to them, knowing that it burns hotter than tobacco, knowing that it has all kinds of chemicals in it, the THC [marijuana potency] level is higher now. Knowing all of that and then educating them of the dangers of putting that into their bodies, and what the future could hold for them then, having done that to themselves. Then I want them to make the choice, but I want them to see through education.

Do you ever feel like there is sort of two different sides of America with regard to drugs?

Brett Richardson: Well, Warsaw [Indiana] is a really conservative community, so you're not going to find many people willing to be outspoken in support of marijuana use in our community. There are people out there, I'm sure, that would favor legalization, and they use it everyday, and they say, "Look at me and I'm fine," and so on.

But being a conservative community as we are, you're not going to find them to be outspoken, [and] we don't go up against any adversaries publicly. We know it's there when you have a sixth-grader come up to you and tell you that mom and dad smoke it all the time. That's apparently acceptable in that family for those parents. Yes, I'm sure we've got both sides, the mirror right there, but hopefully we've got the kids seeing it from our side [and] understanding the dangers of that drug.

People Who Smoke Marijuana Should Get Jail Time

What do you think of the sentencing for this kid's parents when they get busted? Do you think that sentences for marijuana growing are adequate? Too severe? Not severe enough?

Brett Richardson: I don't know that jail time is going to change anything in that person's life. I, of course, do not put mom or dad smoking marijuana at the same level of someone going out and killing somebody or raping someone. So the punishment shouldn't be the same.

But then I've seen video tapes of police officers killed in the line of duty because they stopped a car that has marijuana in it and the people don't want to be arrested. I have mixed emotions about the punishment level. If you're using marijuana, then you're supporting that behavior of people shooting cops.

So, my approach goes right along with the D.A.R.E.'s belief—we can attack the demand side of it, reduce the demand.

It's like any product—you make the product and nobody wants to buy it, you're gonna quit trying to sell it. We do have to punish people who break the law. There has to be some form of punishment. If that means big fines and taking money out of their pocket, do it that way. Some jail time, absolutely. They need to know there are going to be consequences to their choice of using that drug. Lock them away for twenty years? Probably not, but there should be some jail time and definitely some fines.

I've heard of people getting life sentences for growing.

Leann Richardson: Well, as far as what each person gets, it's going to be based on what they have done in regards to marijuana, whether they've grown it or sold it or used it or possessed it. It's illegal for anybody to be involved with marijuana in any way. And as far as the fines or the amount of jail time each person gets, it's going to vary with each separate case. I would hope that the judge would do the right thing, but that's not up to us and we're pretty much law enforcement so we can just do our job to try to get it off the street and educate the kids and leave the other part up to the judges and the people that are in the legislative branch of the government to make the laws that hopefully are right.

> *"Instead of telling kids the truth about [marijuana] . . . DARE officers are free to say what they like, and . . . fill kids' heads with lies and horror stories."*

D.A.R.E. Is Destructive and Ineffective

Dan Savage

In the following viewpoint Dan Savage maintains that the Drug Abuse Resistance Education program (D.A.R.E.) persuades children to turn in their marijuana-smoking parents, which ultimately destroys families. Savage also contends that D.A.R.E. exaggerates marijuana's harmfulness. Worse, Savage charges, D.A.R.E. does not deter cannabis use; one study actually found that D.A.R.E. graduates were more likely to use drugs in high school than those who had not taken the prevention classes. Dan Savage has authored several books and articles.

As you read, consider the following questions:
1. What two important facts were missing from news reports about Aaron Palmer, in Savage's view?
2. What comparison does Keith Stroup make when discussing D.A.R.E. graduates who turn in their parents?
3. According to Savage, what happened to the Tuckers after their sixteen-year-old daughter turned her mother in for smoking marijuana?

Dan Savage, "Dope," *The Stranger*, vol. 11, May 16, 2002. Copyright © 2002 by TheStranger.com. Reproduced by permission of the author.

After a teenager in Covington, Washington, turned his father in for growing marijuana, local TV news reporters and daily newspapers fell all over themselves calling him a hero. Was I the only pot-smoking parent who was horrified?

KIRO 7 Eyewitness News reporter Karen O'Leary does sanctimonious piety better than anyone else in local television news—and that's saying something. As a group, TV news reporters excel at sanctimonious piety, especially when a story involves drugs. Last week [May 9, 2002] O'Leary, a.k.a. Our Lady of the Pursed Lips, reported on "a drug bust turned into a family affair." Aaron Palmer of Covington, Washington, was turned in to the police by his 17-year-old son for growing pot in his garage.

"Neighbors say the kid is responsible and hardworking, a member of the ROTC [Reserve Officers' Training Corps] program," the scowling O'Leary intoned at the beginning of KIRO's coverage. Palmer was arrested late Tuesday night [May 7, 2002] and O'Leary was on the air Thursday with an exclusive interview with Trevor, "[who] told me about his gut-wrenching decision and the fallout from it."

DARE's Teachings

Cut to Trevor, the busted dad's clean-cut 17-year-old son. Trevor showed O'Leary and her camera crew around his father's garage, the spot where his father was allegedly growing pot.

"It's messed-up," Trevor said, complaining about the King County cops who busted his father, tearing his house apart in the process. "They trashed it too thrashed."

Apparently no one warned Trevor that cops called out on a drug bust don't tiptoe through the grow room, or any other room in a suspect's house. Like all kids his age in Covington, Trevor is likely to be a "graduate" of Drug Awareness Resistance Education (DARE), a class taught by smiling uniformed police officers. In DARE classes, cops tell kids that marijuana destroys lives, people who smoke marijuana need help, and cops are the good guys who can provide that help. DARE doesn't warn kids that calling the police on their own parents—as DARE graduates all over the country have done—can result in their homes being torn apart.

Trevor shook his head and looked grim.

"It was affecting his behavior. It was starting to take over his life," Trevor said, sounding like a DARE pamphlet.

"One of Trevor's biggest concerns now," O'Leary broke in, "is that he knows his dad will find out that he was the one who turned him in. That's because the sheriff's department reported it in a press release."

"He's going to blame me," said Trevor, who does a pretty good version of sanctimonious piety himself. "It's one of those fatherhood things. You want your kids to look up to you, not turn you in."

"A very strong young man," O'Leary said at the end of her report.

The Media Portrays Only One Side of the Story

There's so much wrong with the story of the Covington teenager who turned in his dad for growing pot that I hardly know where to begin. O'Leary's performance on KIRO seems as good a place as any to start: People who work in mainstream media like to brag about their objectivity, their fair and balanced reporting. Over here in the alternative press, we get both sides of a story but we're allowed to take positions . . . and we're not afraid to grind our favored axes . . . , unlike the men and women at daily papers and on television news broadcasts who pride themselves on being objective and balanced.

Except when it comes to drugs.

O'Leary's reporting on KIRO was a lot of things—hysterical, melodramatic, sensationalistic—but balanced wasn't one of them. The police said Aaron Palmer had "at least 40 plants," "bags of dried and ready-to-sell marijuana," and "scales to measure the crop."

But Aaron Palmer's lawyer disputes the police account. "Forty plants is a gross exaggeration of the actual number of plants recovered or seized," said Lisa Podell, the criminal defense attorney representing Aaron Palmer. Also missing from O'Leary's report was the reason why Aaron Palmer was growing pot. "Mr. Palmer uses marijuana for medicinal purposes," Podell told me. "He's got bad arthritis, knee problems, and back problems." Palmer's doctors were aware that he was using marijuana to treat his pain, according to Podell. Also missing from O'Leary's report was the fact that Washington state voters approved a medical marijuana initiative in 1998.

Confronted with a chilling account of a kid turning in his own father to the police, KIRO, KING 5, KOMO, Q13, and both daily papers stuck to the drug war script: People who use pot, very bad; people who grow pot, even worse. Aaron Palmer, Drug Lord. His son Trevor, Brave Young Man. If the cops say it was a commercial operation, it was a commercial operation. If the police praise a teenager for turning in his parent, then turning in your parents for having pot in the house is praiseworthy. The mainstream media is terrified of deviating from the drug war script, but is it too much to ask the mainstream media to get its facts straight? For instance, *The Seattle Times* reported that Aaron Palmer had been previously convicted of a drug felony, which isn't true, according to Palmer's lawyer. . . .

DARE Encourages Kids to Turn in Their Parents

[Keith] Stroup [director of the National Organization for the Reform of Marijuana Laws] told me of other cases in which children turned in their parents for growing or smoking pot.

"These thing are always sad," said Stroup. "When I hear of one of these cases where a child turns in his parent, I'm distressed by the damage done to the family." Fifty-seven years old, Stroup went to grade school during some of the darkest moments of the Cold War. "We were constantly told how bad it was in the Soviet Union," said Stroup, "and one of the things that was so awful about the Soviet Union was that Soviet kids were encouraged to report their parents to the police. A police officer was quoted in regards to the Covington story saying that the kid 'did the right thing.' Similar things were no doubt said about children in the Soviet Union who got their parents arrested. The result is, you've got a single father locked up, and a family fractured forever. It's hard to imagine why this should be the case. Who's been helped by this?"

Like me, Stroup suspects that Aaron Palmer's son was exposed to DARE propaganda at an impressionable age. Seven years ago, when Trevor was in fifth grade, the schools in Covington had DARE programs.

"A law-enforcement officer comes into a fifth-grade classroom and tells children how bad marijuana is," said Stroup. "DARE tends to place a special emphasis on marijuana, since that is the drug school-age children are most likely to experiment with."

DEBATING CONTINUED USE OF THE DARE PROGRAM

Anderson. © 2001 by Kirk Anderson. Reproduced by permission.

Instead of telling kids the truth about the drug—the truth is far too positive . . . —DARE officers are free to say what they like, and many, if not most, fill kids' heads with lies and horror stories: Marijuana is addictive; smoke marijuana on Monday and you'll be addicted to heroin by Thursday; all marijuana users wind up in jail; pot will ruin your life.

"Then they ask kids to be on the lookout for things in their own homes," said Stroup. "Every year in this country, a handful of kids, many meaning well, find rolling papers or a roach clip in their parents' rooms, and they become frightened to death that their parents are drug addicts, and they turn their parents in to the 'friendly' officer who lectured them about the dangers of drugs."

An Unpleasant Surprise

The DARE kids who turn their parents in to the police—some have been as young as 10—expect their parents to get a lecture from a friendly DARE officer about the dangers of marijuana, just like they did at school.

"What the parents get, however, is arrested," said Stroup. "People who are good parents—good parents who happen to smoke marijuana—have lost custody of their children. Families have been torn apart."

Kitty Tucker's family was torn apart in 1999 when her 16-year-old daughter turned her in to the police for growing marijuana in her home. Tucker and her family lived in Takoma Park, Maryland, a suburb of Washington, D.C., and one morning she had a confrontation with her daughter. The girl had stayed out all night, so her mother grounded her. Furious, Tucker's daughter called the police to retaliate. "My daughter was scolded for misbehavior," Tucker told me on the phone from her home, "so she called the cops, thinking they would scold us."

"Our home was invaded by policemen without a warrant," said Tucker, "and they took away my plants." Tucker suffers from debilitating migraines and a painful neurological disorder called fibromyalgia, and smoked marijuana to treat her pain. Tucker's husband, who didn't smoke marijuana, was fired from his job with the Department of Energy. Both were prosecuted for growing marijuana. Tucker and her husband eventually pleaded guilty to a misdemeanor, and were placed on probation.

A Teen's Revenge?

Four years ago [in 1998], when I was about to adopt my son, I worried that he would wind up in DARE classes when he reached the fifth grade. What if he found out I occasionally smoked pot and turned me in? What if he found pot growing in the basement of some friend's house and turned the friend in? Thankfully, in the last four years DARE programs have fallen from favor. Research into DARE's programs found them to be ineffective at best. A University of Kentucky study found that DARE had no measurable impact on later drug use; a six-year study at the University of Illinois found that children who had been subjected to DARE's scare tactics were *more* likely to use drugs in high school than kids who hadn't. The Seattle Police Department got out of the DARE program in 1998; Covington Elementary School (part of the Kent School District) dropped out of DARE two years ago. Of course, DARE might not be to blame. Trevor is a 17-year-old high-school senior after all, not a 10-year-old fifth grader. It could be that Aaron Palmer's son, like Kitty Tucker's daughter, was simply pissed at his dad for something and called the cops out of spite. The mainstream reporters in Seattle were too busy falling all over themselves praising Trevor to pause and consider his motives. Couldn't he be a vengeful adolescent lashing out at his full-time parent? . . .

Watching Trevor on the news, I wanted to reach through the television set and choke him. Trevor was the picture of the preening, tormented adolescent, equal parts self-righteousness and self-pity.

"This sucks," Trevor told Q13 news. "Everyone I'm related to thinks I'm the bad guy. But everyone else . . . thinks I'm a hero."

The Truth About Trevor's Action

Not everyone outside your family thinks you're a hero, Trevor. Sure, the *Seattle Post-Intelligencer* published an editorial on Monday [May 13, 2002] praising your bravery and suggesting that "a local civic or service organization" offer you a scholarship . . . but there are a lot of us out here who think you're a complete asshole. Oh, there may be situations in which a father or a son or a brother is morally obligated to turn in a family member: The father of Luke Helder, the Midwestern smiley-face pipe bomber, did the right thing; David Kaczynski did the right thing when he helped lead the police to his brother Ted, the Unabomber. But in both those instances lives were at stake.

Despite what you were told in your DARE classes, Trevor, your dad wasn't hurting anyone—not even himself. All your dad was doing, Trevor, was growing some pot—harmless, non-addictive pot. He wasn't forcing it on you, your siblings, or anyone else. Although what your dad was doing was against the law, the law in this case is unjust and idiotic. We have a moral right to resist and break unjust laws, something they may not have covered in your ROTC classes.

"He's going to blame me, I know it," Trevor whined.

Yeah, well, I suppose so. You are the one who called the cops on your father, after all. Who's he supposed to blame? . . . You could've called your mother, you could've moved out. If you felt your dad was smoking too much dope, you could've called some of his friends over to stage an intervention. There were other options. But you called the cops, turned in your dad, and then watched as cops burst into your home, tore the place apart, and hauled your father—and your 15-year-old sister's father, and your seven-year-old brother's father—away. Your dad was a single parent; while you're old enough to be on your own, your seven-year-old brother isn't. So you not only forever [ruined] your relationship with your father, but you may have [screwed] your siblings out of a father. Nice work, Trev.

Maybe the DARE people will send you a T-shirt.

"The [anti-marijuana public service announcement] campaigns . . . resulted in significant reductions in current marijuana use."

Anti-Marijuana Public Service Announcements Deter Drug Use

National Institute on Drug Abuse

In the following viewpoint the National Institute on Drug Abuse (NIDA) claims that commercials denouncing the use of marijuana can positively influence the behavior of adolescent sensation seekers, who are most likely to use drugs. Anti-marijuana public service announcements (PSAs) targeted to this group, NIDA declares, cause a significant reduction in teen marijuana use. What's more, the organization points out, the effects of PSAs are long-lasting. NIDA is part of the National Institutes of Health in the U.S. Department of Health and Human Services.

As you read, consider the following questions:
1. What is sensation seeking, in Philip Palmgreen's contention?
2. According to NIDA, when were anti-marijuana PSAs aired in Tennessee?
3. How did researchers evaluate the effectiveness of the PSAs, according to the authors?

National Institute on Drug Abuse, "Research Shows TV PSAs Effective in Reducing Teen Marijuana Use," *NIDA News Release*, January 31, 2001.

R esearchers have demonstrated that television public service announcements (PSAs) designed for and targeted to specific teen personality-types can significantly reduce their marijuana use. In a study published in the February 2001 issue of the *American Journal of Public Health*, researchers report that PSAs with an anti-marijuana use message resulted in at least a 26.7 percent drop in the use of that drug among the targeted teen population.

"This study shows that public health messages can have a significant impact if they are prepared and delivered appropriately," says Dr. Alan I. Leshner, Director, National Institute on Drug Abuse (NIDA).

The PSAs were designed to appeal to the 50 percent of teens who tested high (above the median) on sensation seeking. Teens with this personality trait are much more at risk for using drugs, and for using drugs at an earlier age, than are adolescents who test low as sensation seekers.

SENTAR Works for Sensation-Seeking Teens

Dr. Philip Palmgreen, head of the University of Kentucky research team that conducted the study, said that sensation seeking is a "personality trait associated with the need for novel, emotionally intense stimuli and the willingness to take risks to obtain such stimulation."

He and his colleagues used this trait as the basis for developing SENTAR, a prevention approach targeted at sensation seekers. SENTAR encompasses several components, including designing high-sensation-value prevention messages that are novel, dramatic, and attention-getting, and placing these messages in high-sensation-value contexts, such as TV programs that are favorites of high sensation seekers. This study shows that not only does a SENTAR-based campaign get the attention of high sensation seeking teens, but that such campaigns can also change their drug use behaviors.

As part of the study, anti-marijuana PSAs developed for adolescent high sensation seekers were televised January through April 1997 in Fayette County (which includes the city of Lexington), Kentucky. Similar campaigns were conducted January through April 1998 in both Fayette County

The National Youth Anti-Drug Media Campaign Deters Marijuana Use

Teens who have received regular exposure to all or most of the ads in the ONDCP's [Office of National Drug Control Policy's] campaign tend to have more favorable opinions about the effectiveness of anti-drug commercials and indicate less willingness to try drugs. This impact appears to cut across all categories of teens—younger and older, users and non-users, all ethnicities. While the campaign is impacting its intended target, it appears to be having even greater influence on middle school kids.

Among the key target groups, 14–16 year olds and 9th–11th graders, teens who have regularly seen more than half of the ONDCP ads are nearly twice as likely as teens with less exposure to say they have learned a lot about drug risks from TV commercials.

Although older teens are the primary target for the campaign, middle school kids who have received regular exposure to most of the ads in the campaign are more likely than older teens with equal exposure to the ads to say that anti-drug commercials have made them more aware of drug risks, given them new information about drugs, or made them less likely to use drugs.

The ONDCP campaign has likely played a role in educating both marijuana users and non-users about the risks associated with drugs. Regardless of teens' marijuana usage habits, data suggest a correlation between regular viewership of ONDCP ads and teens' perceptions of learning about drug risks from TV commercials.

Adolescents regularly exposed to the ONDCP anti-marijuana commercials are considerably more likely than those who have not been exposed to perceive regular use of marijuana as risky.

About six in ten (61.7%) adolescents who have regularly seen more than half of the ONDCP anti-marijuana commercials say there is a *great* risk involved in using marijuana regularly, compared with only about half (53.2%) of youth who have not been regularly exposed to any of the commercials.

Roper ASW, *Partnership Attitude Tracking Study 2003 Teens Study: Survey of Teens' Attitudes and Behaviors Toward Marijuana*, August 2003.

and Knox County (which includes the city of Knoxville), Tennessee. The PSAs were placed in programs that survey results had indicated are watched by high sensation seeking adolescents. An average of 777 paid spots and 1,160 unpaid spots were aired per campaign. At least 70 percent of the targeted age group was exposed to a minimum of three PSAs a week.

Assessing the Effectiveness of Anti-Marijuana PSAs

To establish the extent of teen marijuana use prior to the campaigns and to assess the effect of the campaigns, 100 randomly selected public school students were interviewed each month in each county for 32 months. The interviews started 8 months before the first Fayette campaign and ended 8 months after the last campaign. The teens were in grades 7 through 10 at the time of the initial interviews. In total, more than 3,000 teens were interviewed in each county.

Pre-exposure levels of marijuana use and other substances by 8th, 10th, and 12th graders in both counties were found to be consistent with figures reported by NIDA's annual Monitoring the Future (MTF) study. For example, 25.5 percent of Fayette County and 20.3 percent of Knox County 12th graders had used marijuana in the past 30 days, in line with 1997 and 1998 national MTF 12th grade estimates of 23.7 percent and 22.8 percent.

The campaigns, however, resulted in significant reductions in current marijuana use (defined as use within the past 30 days) by the target population. The campaigns also were successful in reversing the usual trend of more teens beginning to use marijuana as they get older. In Knox County, effects of the campaign still were evident several months after its conclusion. There, the estimated drop in the relative proportion of high sensation seekers using marijuana was 26.7 percent.

As expected, the campaigns had no effect on teens characterized as low sensation seekers, a group that already exhibited low levels of marijuana use.

"While these findings do not indicate that all anti-drug PSAs will produce behavioral change, nor that PSAs alone should be the only avenue to prevention, they do show that SENTAR-based PSAs can play an important role in drug abuse prevention," Dr. Palmgreen concluded.

> "No kid will be dissuaded by these ads from trying marijuana, since the ads are so at odds with nearly everyone's experience with the drug."

Anti-Marijuana Public Service Announcements Are Ineffective

Rich Lowry

Rich Lowry, editor of *National Review*, argues in the following viewpoint that the government's anti-marijuana public service announcements are dishonest. He asserts that youths who recognize the Office of National Drug Control Policy's scare tactics disregard anti-marijuana announcements and continue to use the drug, which he claims is less harmful than alcohol. Interestingly, Lowry points out, when anti-drug commercials began airing in the early 1990s, drug use by minors escalated and has continued to do so since then.

As you read, consider the following questions:
1. According to Lowry, why can't the ONDCP produce more tempered ads about marijuana?
2. How does the author respond to the government's assertions that drug use supports terrorism?
3. What is Lowry's objection to the government's takeover of the antidrug ad campaign from the private sector?

Rich Lowry, "ONDCP's Anti-Marijuana Ad Campaign," www.townhall.com, January 13, 2003. Copyright © 2003 by North American Syndicate. Reproduced by permission.

If you want to see drugs and violence on television, you don't need to bother tuning in to "NYPD Blue" or loading up a game of "Grand Theft Auto: Vice City." You can just watch one of the Office of National Drug Control Policy's [ONDCP's] latest anti-marijuana ads.

Two teenagers in a marijuana-induced haze sit in a family den, foggy with smoke. After some typical silly banter ("your sister is hot"), one of the kids pulls out his father's gun, says it's unloaded, and to prove it, aims at his friend's head and fires.

ONDCP, showing some residual good taste, spares viewers the splattered brains, but we are supposed to learn that smoking pot will kill you. Other spots suggest that smoking pot will get you raped or make you a rapist, prompt you to run over children on bikes, and otherwise transform you into a rampaging beast.

Over-the-Top Propaganda

Thus is the sensationalistic dishonesty of the War on Drugs broadcast for all to see in a saturation-ad campaign coinciding with the NFL playoffs. No kid will be dissuaded by these ads from trying marijuana, since the ads are so at odds with nearly everyone's experience with the drug. But ONDCP can't produce more tempered and truthful ads about pot—because it simply isn't that scary.

There is, of course, an extremely slim chance that someone smoking pot might be shot by his bong-mate. The odds, however, are probably equally great of smoking dope, writing a hit song about it and becoming (at least temporarily) rich and famous—which was Afroman's experience with his 2001 song "Because I Got High."

In fact, alcohol is more likely than pot to be associated with all of the ONDCP tragedy scenarios, since it is a drug that tends to induce aggression rather than passivity. The ONDCP would never admit this because it raises the question of why pot is illegal and alcohol isn't.

Rather than rationalizing drug policy, ONDCP, under the leadership of [President George W.] Bush nominee John Walters, is more interested in demagogy. Last year's ads airing during the [2002] Super Bowl maintained that drug users support terrorism. The illegal markets created by drug pro-

Youth Exposed to Anti-Marijuana Ads Are Still Likely to Use the Drug

The National Youth Anti-Drug Media Campaign was funded by the Congress to reduce and prevent drug use among young people by addressing youth directly as well as indirectly, and by encouraging their parents and other adults to take actions known to affect youth drug use. The major intervention components include television, radio, and other advertising, complemented by public relations efforts including community outreach and institutional partnerships. . . . [One] component of the Campaign [is] the Marijuana Initiative, which began in late fall 2002. . . .

There is little evidence of direct favorable Campaign effects on youth, either for the Marijuana Initiative period or for the Campaign as a whole. The trend data in marijuana use is not favorable, and for the primary target audience, 14- to 16-year-olds, past year use increased from 2000 through 2003, although this increase was already in place before the start of the Marijuana Initiative. However, an independent source of trend information, the Monitoring the Future Survey, showed a decline in use for some age groups. In any case, youth who were more exposed to Campaign messages are no more likely to hold favorable beliefs or intentions about marijuana than are youth less exposed to those messages, both during the Marijuana Initiative period and over the entire course of the Campaign.

Westat and the Annenberg School for Communication, University of Pennsylvania, *Evaluation of the National Youth Anti-Drug Media Campaign: 2003 Report of Findings Executive Summary*, presented to National Institute on Drug Abuse, December 22, 2003.

hibition create this niche for outlaws in the first place, but never mind.

Now the latest batch of ads recall the over-the-top propaganda of the cult-classic movie "Reefer Madness." An honest anti-pot campaign would stipulate that smoking the drug might make you feel a mild euphoria, but ultimately you should have better things to do with your time. No ad campaign will ever say this, which is one reason that they are so roundly disregarded by kids.

The Campaign's Focus on Marijuana

Corporate-funded anti-drug TV ads started running in major buys in the early 1990s, and youth marijuana use took off.

Operating on the theory that if something doesn't work, it should be funded by taxpayers, the federal government essentially took the ad campaign over from the private sector in mid-1990s.

The emphasis on marijuana in the current spots might seem odd, given how benign it is compared to truly dangerous drugs like heroin, but the campaign has a political point. Marijuana is the weak link in the War on Drugs, and the Bush administration is hoping to shore it up.

The Washington, D.C.–based pro-legalization group, National Organization for Reform of Marijuana Laws, has obtained a Nov. 1, 2002, letter from White House aide Scott Burns to prosecutors across the country urging them to crack down on pot, because "no drug matches the threat posed by marijuana."

Drug warriors have long tried to blunt criticism about drug-war overkill by arguing that no one is ever arrested just for using marijuana. That line of argument is apparently inoperative. One of the new ONDCP ads features two kids smoking dope before the cops swoop in to bust them. Here, finally, is an accurate depiction of one of the potential harms of marijuana: Smoking it can get you arrested.

Why that should be the case is one of the great mysteries of the past 70 years.

> "Treatment was effectively implemented
> with [marijuana-abusing] adolescents with
> mixed demographic characteristics . . . as
> well as from different geographic regions."

Treatment Programs for Marijuana Users Are Effective

Susan Sampl and Ronald Kadden

Susan Sampl and Ronald Kadden of the University of Connecticut School of Medicine authored a therapists' guide to treating youth cannabis addicts, from which the following viewpoint is excerpted. They assert that marijuana-dependent youths can quit using the drug in only five therapy sessions. The therapy they recommend is effective for many different people, they claim. Therapy for marijuana abuse combines motivational enhancement therapy, which encourages youths to stop using marijuana; cognitive behavioral therapy to teach them how to cope with situations that encourage marijuana use; and group therapy to provide them with peer feedback and opportunities for role playing.

As you read, consider the following questions:
1. Who should not receive MET/CBT5 treatment, in the authors' contention?
2. What evidence do Sampl and Kadden give for their conclusion that brief treatment of marijuana abusers is as effective as extended treatment?
3. According to the authors, what is essential to the learning process in cognitive behavioral therapy?

Susan Sampl and Ronald Kadden, *Motivational Enhancement Therapy and Cognitive Behavioral Therapy for Adolescent Cannabis Users: 5 Sessions, Cannabis Youth Treatment Series, Volume 1*. Rockville, MD: Center for Substance Abuse Treatment, Substance Abuse and Mental Health Services Administration, 2001.

Although marijuana use has dropped slightly in the past few years, it is still the most widely used and most readily available illicit psychoactive substance in the United States. In 1998, the rate of marijuana use during the month preceding [this] survey was more than twice that of all other drugs combined (8.3 percent vs. 4.0 percent) and higher than the rate of getting drunk (7.7 percent). Moreover, the rates of marijuana use for 8th graders are twice as high as the rates in 1992. The rate of daily use of marijuana is higher than the rate of daily use of alcohol, and that rate has not gone down. Furthermore, similar trends in marijuana use are reported in regional surveys of junior and senior high school students. Marijuana use has historically been inversely related to an adolescent's perceived risk of using it, and currently this perception among 12th graders is at the lowest point since 1982. Unfortunately, these perceptions do not match the facts.

Dangers of Marijuana Dependence

Relative to nonusers, adolescents who used marijuana (and typically alcohol) weekly were 3 to 47 times more likely to have a host of problems including symptoms of dependence, emergency room admissions, dropping out of school, behavioral problems, fighting, non-drug-related legal problems, other legal problems, and being arrested. Unfortunately, fewer than 1 in 10 adolescents with past-year symptoms of dependence received treatment. From 1992 to 1997, the number of adolescents presenting to publicly funded treatment for marijuana problems increased more than 200 percent; in 1997, 81 percent of adolescents admitted had a primary, secondary, or tertiary problem with marijuana. Marijuana is also the leading substance mentioned in adolescent emergency room admissions and autopsy reports and is believed to be one of the major contributing factors to violent deaths and accidents among adolescents; it has been reported to be involved in as many as 30 percent of adolescent motor vehicle crashes, 20 percent of adolescent homicides, 13 percent of adolescent suicides, and 10 percent of other unintentional injuries among adolescents. . . .

MET/CBT5 [Motivational Enhancement Therapy/Cognitive Behavioral Therapy: 5 Sessions] is designed for the treatment of adolescents between the ages of 12 and 18 with problems related to marijuana use, as indicated by one of the following:

- Meeting criteria for cannabis abuse or dependence
- Experiencing problems (including emotional, physical, legal, social, or academic problems) associated with marijuana use
- Using marijuana at least weekly for 3 months.

Although this treatment includes suggestions for addressing both drug and alcohol use, it is not designed for treating adolescents with poly-substance dependence or those who are heavily using other substances as well as marijuana. In the CYT [Cannabis Youth Treatment] study, adolescents were excluded from the study who drank alcohol on 45 or more of the previous 90 days or who used another drug on 13 or more of the previous 90 days.

MET/CBT5 should not be used to treat adolescents

- Requiring a level of care that is higher than outpatient treatment
- With a social anxiety disorder severe enough to prevent participation in group therapy sessions
- With a severe conduct disorder
- With an acute psychological disorder severe enough to prevent full participation in treatment.

In the CYT study, this treatment was effectively implemented with adolescents with mixed demographic characteristics such as race, age, socioeconomic group, and gender, as well as from different geographic regions. When treating clients, therapists need to be culturally aware of and sensitive to the client group so they can provide relevant examples and use language that is understood by the clients in the therapy session. Likely referral sources of potential MET/CBT5 clients are parents, the justice system, school personnel, and medical or mental health care providers. Self-referral is infrequent.

MET/CBT5 is appropriate for use as either an outpatient treatment or early intervention.

MET/CBT5 can be used by organizations that provide outpatient care, including mental health clinics, youth social service agencies, and mental health private practice settings. . . .

Brief Treatment Is as Effective as Extended Treatment

[Psychology professor Robert] Stephens and [social welfare professor Roger] Roffman compared an 18-session relapse prevention support group approach for the treatment of marijuana problems with a 2-session individualized assessment and intervention approach. The latter included a feedback report based on data collected in pretreatment assessments, discussion of the client's marijuana use and related problems using motivational interviewing principles, and development of a plan for change. The results of the study indicated substantial reductions in marijuana use for both active treatments and no evidence of posttreatment differences between the two approaches in terms of abstinence rates, days of marijuana use, severity of problems, or number of dependence symptoms. Although conclusions regarding null differences must be limited, the large sample sizes and the substantial differences in intensity of the treatments argue for an equivalent efficacy of the two conditions. The results suggest that a minimal intervention approach may be more cost-effective for a marijuana-abusing population than an extended group counseling approach. That study, along with others indicating the general effectiveness of brief interventions for some psychiatric disorders and substance abusers, was an important factor in the decision to test relatively brief interventions in large samples of adults (the companion study to this one) and adolescents (this study) at diverse locations nationally.

How Motivational Enhancement Therapy Works

In the addictions field, the search for critical conditions that are necessary and sufficient to induce change has led to the identification of six critical elements:
- Feedback regarding personal risk or impairment
- Emphasis on personal responsibility for change
- Clear advice to change
- A menu of alternative change options
- Therapist empathy
- Facilitation of client self-efficacy or optimism.

Therapeutic interventions containing some or all of these

185

elements have been effective in initiating change and reducing alcohol use.

The MET approach is further grounded in research on processes of change. [Professors James] Prochaska and [Carlo] DiClemente describe five stages of change that people progress through in modifying problem behaviors (the stages of precontemplation, contemplation, determination, action, and maintenance). The MET approach assists clients in moving through the stages toward action and maintenance.

In sum, MET is based on motivational principles and has been utilized increasingly in clinical interventions and research, primarily in the alcoholism field. Recently it has also been included as a component in the study that is a companion to the present one—evaluating brief treatments for adult marijuana abusers.

MET's Usefulness in Treating Marijuana-Dependent Adolescents

The MET sessions included in MET/CBT5 are planned as individual therapy sessions for a number of reasons. First, motivational enhancement therapy is designed to be an individual approach in which the therapist works with each client regarding that client's own specific reasons for considering change. Most previous effective demonstrations of motivational enhancement therapy have utilized an individual therapy format. This individual approach in MET/CBT5 is reflected in the use of a personalized feedback report, which stimulates discussion of that client's personal concerns and motivations regarding his or her substance use. An individual session is most conducive to a personal discussion. In addition, individual MET sessions are preferable because clients may feel embarrassed about aspects of their substance abuse and related problems; initially they may feel more comfortable discussing these problems individually. Finally, adolescent clients sometimes feel apprehensive about verbalizing their motivation to quit marijuana in front of their peers, for fear that their peers will think that they are not cool. They may have a better chance of contemplating their ambivalence about quitting—and firming up their motivation to address their marijuana use—by working with the therapist privately at first.

Sequence of MET/CBT5 Treatment

Session	Modality	Time Period	Primary Approach	Topics
1	Individual	60 min.	MET	Rapport and motivation building. Review of personalized feedback report.
2	Individual	60 min.	MET	Goal setting. Introduction to functional analysis. Preparation for group sessions.
3	Group	75 min.	CBT	Marijuana refusal skills, with roleplay practice exercises.
4	Group	75 min.	CBT	Enhancing social support network. Increasing pleasant activities.
5	Group	75 min.	CBT	Coping with unanticipated high-risk situations and relapses.

Susan Sampl and Ronald Kadden, *Motivational Enhancement Therapy and Cognitive Behavioral Therapy for Adolescent Cannabis Users: 5 Sessions, Cannabis Youth Treatment Series, Volume 1.* Rockville, MD: Center for Substance Abuse Treatment, Substance Abuse and Mental Health Services Administration, 2001.

This MET/CBT5 therapy is an adaptation of adult treatment to adolescents. The unique developmental tasks of adolescence play a role in substance use disorders and their treatment. [Joseph] Nowinski's 1990 book, *Substance Abuse in Adolescents and Young Adults: A Guide to Treatment*, provides a useful discussion of substance abuse in relation to adolescent development that may help inform therapists using MET/CBT5. Nowinski discusses the primary adolescent developmental task of individuation, in which adolescents develop identities separate from their parents or caregivers. As a part of this individuation process, adolescents are especially likely to question what adults tell them. Using MET style minimizes the likelihood of provoking resistance, which might occur in a highly directive or confrontational therapeutic approach. As a result, the MET approach seems particularly promising for adolescent marijuana abusers. In MET the therapist works with the client's own marijuana use goal, helping to evaluate the benefits and disadvantages of abstinence versus continued use. This process supports the development of self-control, another key developmental task of adolescence.

The therapists in MET/CBT5 encourage adolescents to try an extended period of abstinence from marijuana to evaluate potential impacts on their lives. In keeping with the MET style though, there is a tolerance for the adolescent's ambivalence about change. The therapist does not try to force abstinence, but helps the client to understand the risks associated with continued use. It is possible that this aspect of MET may be problematic for others in the adolescent's life who may take issue with the therapist not insisting on absolute abstinence. As a matter of fact, many adolescents referred to the treatment may have already been told by other authority figures that they need to abstain from marijuana, with little or no impact on their behavior. It may be that if the therapist were to echo this unilateral message, it too would have little therapeutic impact. It may be useful to educate those in supportive roles around the adolescent client about this aspect of MET to decrease the likelihood that they will react negatively and undermine the therapist's credibility.

Why Cognitive Behavioral Therapy Is Needed

Cognitive behavioral therapy (CBT) is designed to remediate deficits in skills for coping with antecedents to marijuana use. Individuals who rely primarily on marijuana (or other substances) to cope have little choice but to resort to substance use when the need to cope arises. The goal of this intervention is to provide some basic alternative skills to cope with situations that might otherwise lead to substance use. Skill deficits are viewed as central to the relapse process; therefore, the major focus of the CBT groups will be on the development and rehearsal of skills.

The cognitive-behavioral treatment approach used in this intervention is based on that described in *Treating Alcohol Dependence: A Coping Skills Training Guide*, a treatment manual that focuses on training in interpersonal and self-management skills. It incorporates treatment elements that have demonstrated clinical effectiveness with alcoholic clients into a manual of interventions aimed at adolescents that can be reliably delivered, monitored, and evaluated.

The focus of CBT treatment is on teaching and practicing overt behaviors, while attempting to keep cognitive demands on clients to a minimum. Repetition is essential to the learning process in order to develop proficiency and to ensure that newly acquired behaviors will be available when needed. Therefore, behavioral rehearsal will be emphasized, using varied, realistic case examples to enhance generalization to real life settings. During the rehearsal periods, clients are asked to identify cues that signal high-risk situations, indicating their recognition of when to employ newly learned coping skills.

The Importance of Group Therapy

Many of the problems or skill deficits associated with substance abuse are interpersonal in nature, and the context of a group provides a realistic yet "safe" setting for the acquisition or refinement of new skills. A number of features associated with group approaches to treatment may facilitate cognitive, affective, and behavioral changes. These factors include the realization that others share similar problems; development of social behaviors; opportunity to try out new behaviors in a safe environment; and development and enhancement of interpersonal learning and trust. Group therapy breaks through clients' isolation, encouraging development of interdependence and identification with other marijuana users, while at the same time avoiding overdependence on the therapist. It also provides the therapist with an opportunity to observe the interpersonal behavior of each group member.

With respect to social skills training, important aspects of the treatment, particularly modeling, rehearsal, and feedback, probably occur more powerfully in a group setting. A client model whose skill level is only somewhat greater than that of a peer observer is likely to have more impact than a skilled therapist is.

A group-therapy format also provides opportunities for behavioral rehearsal and risk taking. Clients benefit from feedback offered by their peers, from discussions of anticipated obstacles to implementation of new skills, and from the case examples provided by fellow clients. There is also the possibility for greater habituation of social anxiety in a group setting. Group therapy is the most widely used form of treatment delivery for substance abuse rehabilitation. It has a high level of clinical relevance and can be utilized across a variety of treatment settings (e.g., inpatient, outpatient, day programs). Therefore, the results of any study using group therapy are likely to have an impact on current practice. Group therapy is also likely to have a bright future in these increasingly cost-conscious times because of its favorable client-to-staff ratio.

Group therapy can be a particularly powerful modality for teen clients given the importance of peer influence in adolescence. Feedback from a peer is likely to have greater impact on adolescent clients than similar feedback from the therapist. In the group CBT sessions, therapists encourage adolescent participants to offer other group members positive and constructive feedback.

"After all this propaganda about what a big problem marijuana addiction supposedly is, it can be successfully 'treated' with 'just two individual sessions with a trained therapist.'"

Treatment Programs for Marijuana Users Are Unnecessary

Richard Cowan

Sending marijuana users to treatment programs is pointless, argues Richard Cowan in the following viewpoint. He argues that the drug is rarely addictive. As proof that marijuana users do not need extensive treatment, Cowan points to studies that found simple incentive programs can convince heavy cannabis users to quit. He reasons that if a marijuana user can be convinced to quit simply by undergoing two treatment sessions, the individual is obviously not addicted. Cowan is editor and publisher of *Marijuana News*.

As you read, consider the following questions:

1. In the 2000 NHSDA, what were the criteria for marijuana dependence as cited by Cowan?
2. How does Cowan respond to the government's argument that marijuana can be addictive for some people?
3. What does the author say about the decreasing number of teens who smoke cigarettes?

The Sunday [December 15, 2002] *New York Times* printed a letter from [drug czar] John Walters that made my day with something new. His letter had the standard line, "Marijuana now surpasses heroin as a reason for an emergency visit." I have dealt [with] that many times.

The Government's Contradictions

That lie dates back at least to [former secretary of Health and Human Services] Donna Shalala, and it gets boring after a while.

However, he also introduced a new one, claiming, "The increase in the number of people needing treatment for marijuana is not a function of 'more aggressive law enforcement.' The data derive from applying the diagnostic criteria of the American Psychiatric Association to responses from the National Household Survey of Drug Abuse [NHSDA]."

Of course, that contradicts the statements on the government's own web site: "By 1999, more than half of all adolescent marijuana admissions were referred through the criminal justice system. Adolescent marijuana admissions through the criminal justice system increased at a higher rate than admissions through other sources."

I have dealt with that as well.

But the reference to the "diagnostic criteria of the American Psychiatric Association" was something new!

So I read what the National Household Survey of Drug Abuse said about that. If we had any doubt about the total corruption of science by cannabis prohibition, this should end it.

Here is how it works [according to the Substance Abuse and Mental Health Services Administration]:

DSM-IV [Diagnostic and Statistical Manual of Mental Disorders, Fourth ed.] defines a person as dependent if he or she met three out of seven dependence criteria (for substances with a withdrawal criterion) or three out of six criteria (for substances without a withdrawal criterion). . . .

An additional criterion for marijuana in the 2000 NHSDA, but not in prior years, is that a person must have used marijuana on 6 or more days to be defined as dependent on marijuana. . . .

Persons who received specialty treatment in the past year but did not meet the criteria for dependence or abuse were included in the definition of treatment need because it was assumed that if a person received treatment, he or she probably needed it at some point in the past year.

Among the persons who received specialty treatment in the past year but did not meet the criteria for dependence or abuse, 53.2 percent were still in some kind of treatment at the time of interview, 27.9 percent had successfully completed treatment, 28.1 were arrested and booked in the past year, and 41.1 percent were on probation, parole, or other conditional release at some time in the past year.

In other words, if you were sent to "treatment" by the courts or school or by anyone else without a diagnosis of "dependence or abuse", you must need treatment even though you don't otherwise "meet the criteria for dependence or abuse." By definition.

We could not make this up, but they did.

So where does this lead us?

Any Substance Can Be Addictive

Consider this [statement by the National Institute on Drug Abuse (NIDA)]:

Is marijuana use addictive?

Long-term marijuana use can lead to addiction for some people, that is, they use the drug compulsively even though it often interferes with family, school, work, and recreational activities. According to the 1999 National Household Survey on Drug Abuse, of the 4.7 million Americans age 12 and older needing treatment for drug abuse, 2.8 million were having problems with marijuana or hashish. In 1998, more than 208,000 people entering drug abuse treatment programs reported that marijuana was their primary drug of abuse.

While the circular argument continues, they touch upon a topic that is generally avoided in the addiction context, obsessive/compulsive behavior. "Long-term marijuana use can lead to addiction for some people, that is, they use the drug compulsively. . . ." Obviously anything can become compulsive, including handwashing. Would it make sense to say, "Long term use of hand soap can become addictive for some people"—and then blame the soap?

In fact, obsessive/compulsive behaviors, most notably gambling and eating disorders, are a much bigger problem than substance abuse—other than alcoholism and tobacco use—

193

would be without prohibition. However, the quacks in the re-hab rackets depend on the Drug War ideology for their justi-fication, so everything that is not chemical is ignored or treated with physically addictive pharmaceuticals like Prozac.

Marijuana Treatment Is Short and Simple

But what is the "treatment" for cannabis "addicts?" It gets even better. [According to NIDA,]

> Treatment programs directed specifically at marijuana abuse are rare, partly because many individuals who use marijuana do so in combination with other drugs, such as cocaine and alcohol. However, with more people now seeking help specifically to control marijuana abuse, research has sharp-ened its focus on ways to overcome problems associated with abuse of this drug.

One study [cited by NIDA] suggests that brief treatment, consisting of just two individual sessions with a trained ther-apist can reduce marijuana use by 70 percent. In these 90-minute individual sessions, the therapist uses motivational interviewing techniques, which reinforce patients' desires to quit, and discusses strategies that patients can use to avoid or overcome the temptation to use marijuana. This brief ap-proach was found to be as effective as a much longer group therapy. Another study suggests that giving patients vouch-ers that they can redeem for goods—such as movie passes,

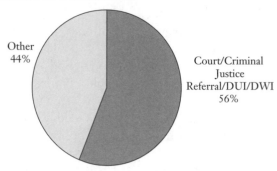

Primary Source of Referral for Marijuana Treatment Admissions

Other
44%

Court/Criminal
Justice
Referral/DUI/DWI
56%

Substance Abuse and Mental Health Services Administration, Treatment Episode Data Set, 1997–1999.

194

sporting equipment, or vocational training—may further improve outcomes.

I once asked a very knowledgeable Dutch friend about the treatment for "cannabis addicts" in Holland, where there is little in the way of coercion, and he said that mostly it consisted of talking to them a bit. That is usually all it takes.

A similar if longer version seems to work even on VERY heavy cannabis users.

So, after all this propaganda about what a big problem marijuana addiction supposedly is, it can be successfully "treated" with "just two individual sessions with a trained therapist." Try that at an AA meeting or tell that to a friend who is trying to quit tobacco! On second thought, don't.

And, oh, yes, throw in a few movie passes and it works better still.

This [marijuana] is what Walters has called "two-thirds of the addiction problem in America today."

Even though just talking to people can supposedly "reduce marijuana use by 70 percent," the same [NIDA] web page says, "Currently, no medications are available to treat marijuana abuse. However, recent discoveries about the workings of [marijuana] receptors have raised the possibility that scientists may eventually develop a medication that will block the intoxicating effects of [marijuana]. Such a medication might be used to prevent relapse to marijuana abuse by reducing or eliminating its appeal."

They want to give a drug to stop people from using a plant that people can stop using if offered movie passes.

The Use of Dangerous Drugs Is Increasing

On a related note, the [2002] Monitoring the Future teen drug use survey was published, and there was the usual media parroting of the party line.

As always, the emphasis was on cannabis, but, as the *New York Times* reported, "One of the biggest declines occurred in smoking, with the proportion of teenagers who said that they had ever smoked cigarettes falling by 4 or 5 percentage points compared with 2001 in each of the three grades, 8th, 10th and 12th."

Of course, no adults were arrested for tobacco possession

to produce those excellent results. In fact, the much smaller reported drop in teen cannabis use was probably within the margin of error, which was not reported. That is not new.

What was new was the addition of numbers on Oxycontin and Vicodin. Marijuana use supposedly dropped a bit but, "Oxycontin use in the past year without a doctor's orders was reported by 1.3 percent of 8th graders, 3.0 percent of 10th graders, and 4.0 percent of 12th graders. Nonmedical use of Vicodin in the past year was reported by 2.5 percent of 8th graders, 6.9 percent of 10th graders, and 9.6 percent of 12th graders."

Almost 10 percent of twelfth graders have used Vicodin, the drug of choice at Betty Ford and other celebrity rehab centers. And heroin use remained unchanged. What a triumph!

"This survey confirms that our drug prevention efforts are working and that when we work together and push back, the drug problem gets smaller," says Walters.

It must be true, by definition.

| *"DEA's marijuana eradication activities resulted in the eradication of 3.6 million cultivated marijuana plants, the execution of 8,480 arrests, and the seizure of $25 million in assets."*

The Government's Marijuana Suppression Program Reduces Drug Use

Karen Tandy

In March 2004 Karen Tandy, administrator of the U.S. Drug Enforcement Administration (DEA), gave a speech before the U.S. House of Representatives, from which the following viewpoint is excerpted. In it she contends that the DEA's marijuana suppression plan reduces the drug's availability and has resulted in the arrests of people who lead marijuana trafficking organizations, operate grow rooms, and harvest marijuana on federal land. Declining cannabis use among youths, Tandy maintains, can be attributed in part to the DEA's efforts.

As you read, consider the following questions:
1. In Tandy's opinion, who controls cultivation of domestic marijuana?
2. What were the three results of the DEA's efforts in 2003, as cited by the author?
3. According to Tandy, what did the DEA observe at an Ohio warehouse?

Karen Tandy, statement before the U.S. House Subcommittee on Commerce, Justice, State, the Judiciary, and Related Agencies, Committee on Appropriations, Washington, DC, March 24, 2004.

The President's National Drug Control Strategy has made a difference. The most recent *Monitoring the Future Survey* [published in 2003] shows that overall drug use by our youth is down 11 percent, exceeding the President's two-year goal of reducing youth drug use by 10 percent. It is the first significant downturn in youth drug use in nearly a decade, with reductions in drug use noted among 8th, 10th, and 12th graders, and levels of use for some drugs that are lower than they have been in almost three decades. Current MDMA [Ecstasy] use is down by more than half, marijuana use is down 11 percent, and amphetamine use (including methamphetamine) fell by 17 percent.

Despite these successes, DEA's [Drug Enforcement Agency's] most recent Domestic Threat Assessment highlights the many challenges we are still facing. In 2002, an estimated 19.5 million Americans—8.3 percent of the population age 12 or older—were current illicit drug users. I would like to take this opportunity to discuss these domestic threats and how DEA makes a difference in reducing the availability of illicit drugs in America.

Marijuana Trafficking Is a Major Problem

Marijuana continues to be a significant threat given its popularity and availability. Americans spend more than $10.4 billion every year on marijuana. Recent supply availability estimates indicate that between 10,000 and 24,000 pure metric tons of marijuana are available in the United States. The 2002 National Survey on Drug Use and Health (NSDUH), formerly called the National Household Survey on Drug Abuse (NHSDA), found that marijuana was the most commonly used illicit drug with 14.6 million users during the past month. This represents a statistically significant increase in the use of marijuana between CY [calendar year] 2001 and CY 2002 (from 5.4 to 6.2 percent). About one third of the marijuana users (4.8 million) used the drug on 20 or more days in the past month. Marijuana accounted for 119,472 mentions in emergency department visits in CY 2002, second only to cocaine among drug-related visits. Each year, more teens enter treatment for marijuana dependence than for all illicit drugs combined, including alcohol.

Marijuana trafficking is prevalent across the nation, with both domestic and foreign sources of supply. Small, independent operators generally control the indoor and outdoor cultivation of domestic marijuana. Mexican drug trafficking organizations dominate the transportation and wholesale distribution of the majority of foreign-based marijuana available in the United States and are believed to be cultivating marijuana on U.S. public lands throughout California. Traffickers in Mexico move bulk shipments of marijuana through the Southwest Border by land, sea, and air. Drug trafficking organizations based in Colombia and Mexico move shipments of marijuana through the Caribbean to the eastern and southeastern United States on commercial and noncommercial vessels. Canada also has become a substantial source of marijuana smuggled into the United States. Marijuana from Canada, commonly referred to as BC Bud, is now available in every region of the United States. Since the demand for marijuana far exceeds that for any other illegal drug and the profit potential is so high, some cocaine and heroin drug trafficking organizations reportedly traffic marijuana to help finance their drug operations.

The DEA's Marijuana Suppression Program Is Successful

DEA aggressively strives to halt the spread of marijuana cultivation in the United States through the Domestic Cannabis Eradication and Suppression Program (DCE/SP), the only nationwide program that exclusively targets marijuana. DEA continues to improve the effectiveness of its marijuana eradication efforts by spending $12.6 million in CY 2003 to support the 100 state and local agencies that are now active DCE/SP participants. DEA's marijuana eradication activities resulted in the eradication of 3.6 million cultivated marijuana plants, the execution of 8,460 arrests, and the seizure of $25 million in assets in CY 2003. In addition, DEA continues monitoring state legislation to combat marijuana legalization. Where appropriate, DEA provides information to state legislators about the facts concerning marijuana and how proposed legislation impacts on drug law enforcement.

Eight (8) of the 40 "Most Wanted" drug trafficking and

money laundering organizations (20 percent)—CPOTs—engage in marijuana trafficking. As of February 2004, there are 23 active DEA Priority Target investigations linked to these 8 CPOTs. Between FY 2001 and FY 2003, DEA disrupted 28 and dismantled 35 marijuana PTOs [Priority Target Organizations]. As of February 2004, there were 86 open marijuana PTO investigations. DEA's efforts on reducing the availability of marijuana in the United States are evidenced by the following recent success stories:

Markstein. © 1986 by Copley News Service. Reproduced by permission.

• *Operation Enigma*—a Special Operations Division (SOD)-supported, multi-jurisdictional, multi-national OCDETF [Organized Crime Drug Enforcement Task Force] wire intercept operation initiated in January 2001—targeted CPOT Armando Valencia-Cornelio. This Mexico-based, poly-drug trafficking organization is believed to be responsible for the importation and distribution of multi-ton quantities of cocaine and marijuana, and multi-hundred pound quantities of heroin and methamphetamine, in the United States. Specifically, this organization was responsible for the receipt and distribution of approximately 20–30 tons of cocaine on a monthly basis. As of March 2004, *Operation Enigma* has resulted in 214 arrests and the seizure of 1,361 kilograms of cocaine, 43 kilograms of heroin, 38,665 pounds of marijuana, 117 pounds of methamphetamine, 96 weapons, and $8.9 million in U.S. currency. CPOT Valencia-Cornelio was arrested in August 2003.

Marijuana Growers Have Been Indicted Due to DEA's Efforts

• On February 25, 2004, DEA, in cooperation with ATF, discovered a three-level, indoor marijuana "grow" operation behind a concealed entrance in a Youngstown, Ohio warehouse. DEA Agents seized approximately 3,800 marijuana plants in various stages of maturity from seven separate rooms in the warehouse. In production since 2000, the sophisticated indoor operation utilized an automated watering and fertilizing system, as well as extensive artificial lighting, to foster rapid growth of the plants. Intelligence information indicated the operation harvested only the buds of the marijuana plant and shipped two 55 gallon drums of product weekly. Additional plant material was discarded. Prior surveillance at the location had observed the delivery of 15–17 pallet-loads of expensive grow mix. Electric bills for the warehouse during the past year averaged $3,000 per month.

• On February 18, 2004, Rigoberto Gaxiola-Medina and nine additional subjects were indicted in the Judicial District of Arizona as a result of a DEA investigation in cooperation with Mexican authorities. The investigation revealed a close link between Gaxiola-Medina and CPOT Joaquin Guzman-Loera, aka "Chapo." This OCDETF/PTO investigation disrupted a major marijuana trafficking organization operating on both sides of the Southwest Border by eliminating the use of a tunnel for criminal activities. As a result of this investigation, DEA conducted two separate seizures of marijuana totaling approximately 1,237 lbs., which were directly linked to the tunnel. A provisional arrest warrant is being submitted for the arrest and extradition of Gaxiola-Medina.

• On July 2, 2003, DEA's San Francisco Field Division, working with the Placer County Sheriff's Department (PCSO), California Bureau of Narcotic Enforcement (BNE) and the U.S. Forest Service (USFS), seized 3,499 growing marijuana plants at an outdoor grow site in the Forest Hill National Forest, in Placer County, CA. Pedro Villa-Garcia was arrested at the grow site and one other unidentified Hispanic male fled from the scene and was not apprehended. This grow site was previously identified pursuant to a DEA investigation, *Operation Green Wine*. The plants seized from the site were located in a well-traveled area, which likely would have been discovered by the public, and therefore posed a threat to the public's safety. During the interview, Villa-Garcia identified himself as an illegal alien from Michoacan, Mexico brought to the area for the purpose of tending to the crop. Villa-Garcia was booked on California State charges for "cultivation and possession with intent to distribute marijuana." In January 2004, Villa-Garcia was sentenced to 60 months in prison for his involvement with the grow operation.

| *"Tens of thousands of marijuana growers and users have been shot dead, wounded, arrested, incarcerated [by the DEA]. . . . Millions of pounds of cured marijuana have been confiscated and wasted."*

The Government's Marijuana Suppression Program Is Harmful

Pete Brady

In the following viewpoint Pete Brady argues that by acting against marijuana growers, the Drug Enforcement Administration (DEA) is waging a war against individuals, families, and ecosystems. The DEA, Brady asserts, is responsible for the deaths of countless federal agents, marijuana users, and dealers. Additionally, through poisoning cannabis plants, the DEA destroys the environment, he claims. Moreover, he maintains, the DEA's suppression program has not led to a reduction in marijuana use. Pete Brady is a writer and medical marijuana user.

As you read, consider the following questions:

1. What three situations does Brady cite in his claim that the DEA's fingerprints are everywhere?
2. According to the author, what is the DEA's "success disincentive" in winning the drug war?
3. What leads Brady to conclude that the DEA stands for "Dishonest Education Agency"?

During Ronald Reagan's presidency, the [Drug Enforcement Administration (DEA)] teamed with the FBI, CIA, and US military, primarily in operations against international marijuana and cocaine cartels. DEA agent Kiki Camarena, based in Guadalajara, Mexico in 1985, helped the Mexican government destroy ten thousand tons of high-grade sinsemilla [marijuana]. Camarena was then kidnapped, tortured and murdered by Mexicans. The US response to his death, which included kidnapping Mexicans so they could be put on trial in American courts, caused cross-border friction.

DEA activities in Latin American countries were termed "US imperialism" by foreign critics, who often cite a DEA-sponsored 1989 coup that resulted in Panamanian president Manuel Noriega being kidnapped by force from Panama and put on trial in the United States.

Despite such criticism, Congress gave the DEA increased authority for international operations, and also funded a DEA air force—a sophisticated $25 million Texas-based "Air Wing" with a hundred planes capable of specialized surveillance, interdiction, and photography.

Too Much Power

No matter how many drugs seized, no matter how many arrests, DEA officials relentlessly insist that "drug use continues to skyrocket," and that the primary way to combat it is by giving more funding and power to the DEA!

Soon after its creation, the agency began writing legislation that was rubber stamped by Congress, legislation that gives the DEA authority over domestic and international manufacturers, prescribers or retailers of pharmaceutical drugs, chemicals, and steroids.

To counter grassroots drug policy reformers, the DEA teamed with President Reagan, his wife Nancy, and George Bush, to create anti-reform "parents' groups," a "demand reduction program" that tells people all illegal drugs are dangerous, and expensive programs attacking money laundering and steroids, along with harmless chemicals that can be used to make methamphetamine and "club drugs".

Today, the DEA's fingerprints are everywhere—in South American mountain villages where US poison and genetically engineered bioweapons rain from the sky, in American pharmacies inspected by DEA agents, in schools and communities where the DEA infiltrates classrooms and local law enforcement agencies.

The DEA has also increased the suffering of medical marijuana patients. In 1988, the agency's administrative law judge correctly ruled that marijuana had legitimate medical uses and was relatively harmless. In 1989, DEA boss Jack Lawn threw out the judge's ruling. . . .

Untruths Evident in the DEA Museum

[In northern Virginia] the [DEA] museum's overall tone combines dissonant themes. One theme is macho and macabre, embodying a swashbuckling world of pot-laden smuggling planes, gun battles, good (DEA) versus evil (drug traffickers and users), bloodied bodies of dead drug traffickers and valiant DEA martyrs. The exhibit even contains a compact disc of a "Mexican Narcomusic" band called "Grupo Exterminato" that "glorifies drug criminals with ballad songs."

The museum's other theme is that America is under siege—flooded with drugs, plagued by drug users' desire for drugs. Somehow, even though the DEA claims to be a sophisticated, effective agency, drug use is as prevalent as it has ever been, if not moreso.

Perhaps there's a success disincentive built in to the entire drug war equation. If the DEA actually "won" its war, it would need to be downsized, and thousands of well-paid employees would have to get jobs elsewhere. Viewed from the perspective of job security, failure is success.

Marijuana: Always with Us

That's the title of a section in a DEA publication, and the agency has zealously continued [drug war founder Harry] Anslinger's war against weed. The DEA began its Domestic Cannabis Eradication and Suppression Program (DCE/SP) in 1979 in Hawaii and California; today, all 50 states participate in the program, which costs tens of millions of dollars annually.

DEA literature complains that outdoor cannabis growers cause environmental damage using poisons and otherwise harming indigenous flora, but the same literature proudly proclaims that the agency's 1990 Operation Wipe Out in Hawaii used poisons to eradicate 90% of Hawaii's outdoor buds. In Oklahoma and Texas, The DEA spent a month killing 714 gardens containing 40,000 specially bred sinsemilla plants on the banks of the Red River.

After growers moved to indoor gardens and began developing sophisticated botanical skills and precursors to stabilized, high-potency strains now sold by Marc Emery and other seedmeisters, the DEA's Operation Green Merchant moved in on Holland's famous Seed Bank and on the American hydroponics industry in 1989.

Many people busted by Green Merchant were told by the DEA that they had come to the agency's attention solely because they advertised in *High Times* magazine, or because a subpoena had been served on the magazine.

The DEA developed infrared radar to detect "unusual heat signatures" generated by indoor grow rooms, and began busting massive indoor cultivation set-ups like Northern California's "Advance Mine" site, a series of mining caves containing 5 tons of grow equipment and $6 million worth of marijuana.

The DEA's Efforts to Reduce Marijuana Use

The agency's one-time seizure tallies are impressive: it took down 389,113 pounds of herb in Miami in 1988, scored 75,000 pounds of hash in San Francisco that same year, confiscated 4,260,000 pounds of pot during one Mexican bust in 1984, and ripped off 290,400 pounds of hashish in Mexico in 1995. By contrast, the DEA's biggest heroin seizure ever was only 2,816 pounds.

Stats for 1999 indicate that the DEA and its affiliates "eradicated" 3.5 million outdoor plants and 208,000 indoor plants, while arresting 12,000 people and seizing $2.7 million in assets. Just a few months ago, the DEA completed a two-year bust of 120 FedEx employees and associates, who had shipped 121 tons of reefer through the FedEx system, using fake labels, bribes and overnight delivery of more than 4,000 cannabis packages.

The agency sponsors forums teaching cops, parents, and

community groups how to fight medical marijuana and drug policy reform. Its website features an anti-pot book for teenagers called *Get It Straight*. The book says marijuana causes people to have "difficulty understanding simple ideas," and also causes "lung cancer" and immune system deficiencies.

The U.S. Government's Marijuana Eradication Program Is Misguided

The NORML [National Organization for the Reform of Marijuana Laws] Foundation strongly opposes the "aerial directed spraying" of herbicides from low flying aircraft for the purpose of eliminating wild growing marijuana plots. After evaluating the Drug Enforcement Administration's [DEA's] Domestic Cannabis Eradication Suppression Program (DCE/SP), we find it misguided, overly burdensome on taxpayers, counterproductive, and potentially harmful to the health and safety of residents and the environment.

A 1998 Vermont State Auditor's report evaluating the DEA's [Drug Enforcement Administration's] marijuana eradication efforts revealed that over 99 percent of the 422,716,526 total marijuana plants eliminated nationwide by the agency in 1996 were "ditchweed," non-psychoactive hemp. The DEA defines ditchweed as: "Wild, scattered marijuana plants [with] no evidence of planting, fertilizing, or tending.". . . This strain of cannabis presents no threat to public safety because it contains too little THC [marijuana's active ingredient] to intoxicate users. . . .

The Vermont Auditor's report found that the DEA spent over $9 million on marijuana eradication efforts in all 50 states in 1996. (This figure does not include the cost of state and local participation.) . . . The bulk of these taxpayer's dollars were spent eradicating plants that present no threat to public safety. In fact, South Dakota spent $105,000 in 1996 eliminating only ditchweed. States like Missouri, North Dakota, and Illinois engaged in similar activities. In those states, ditchweed comprised more than 99.95 percent of the total plants eradicated by law enforcement at a cost to taxpayers of just under one million dollars.

Paul Armentano, public testimony before the U.S. Department of Agriculture, May 27, 1998.

If you smoke marijuana, the DEA asserts, you will be "unable to perform tasks requiring concentration, like driving, swimming, playing sports, reading and writing."

How odd, I thought, while reading *Get It Straight.* I am a medical marijuana patient with serious spinal injuries. I'm also an ocean swimmer who writes, reads, concentrates, and swims after smoking marijuana.

Is it possible that DEA also stands for "Dishonest Education Agency?"

Pointless Deaths

The DEA's "Association of Former Federal Narcotics Agents" publishes a history of the DEA that reveals more about the agency's flaws and the drug war's contradictions than the former agents likely intended.

In the published history are short autobiographies of agents who died trying to keep people from making, selling or using drugs. The first casualty was a federal alcohol prohibition agent killed by Mexican whiskey smugglers in 1921. In 1922, Narcotics inspector Burt Gregory was killed when his own gun accidentally discharged. In 1924, 25-year-old Agent James Williams was accidentally killed by another agent's gun; it was Williams' first assignment. Agent James Brown, who was known for impersonating Mexican women during undercover ops, was killed by an opium trafficker in 1928.

Inspector Spencer Stafford died in 1935, killed by a Texas sheriff. Mansel Burrell, one of few African-Americans depicted in the DEA [deaths] list, died in 1967 at age 23. Agent Eugene McCarthy was killed in Saudi Arabia in a helicopter accident. Detective Stephen Struel, a Missouri police officer working with a DEA anti-pot team; Charles Bassing, an Arkansas State Police officer; and fellow Arkansas officers James Avant and Kevin Brosch, are among those who died during DEA aerial marijuana surveillance operations.

The sad list goes on and on. Several dozen government anti-drug agents and contract workers—most of them under 40—have been killed since America began experimenting with prohibition.

Their lost lives echo the pain and loss of other individuals, families, and ecosystems. People who grow, process, transport and use coca, peyote, mushrooms and opiates around the world have been gunned down or set up by the DEA.

Tens of thousands of marijuana growers and users have been shot dead, wounded, arrested, incarcerated. Millions of marijuana plants, which could have provided food, fuel, fiber, fun, have been hacked down, incinerated, poisoned. Millions of pounds of cured marijuana have been confiscated and wasted.

Ironies Abound

In the introduction to a DEA publication, Public Information Officer Robert Feldkamp recalls the good old days, when DEA was housed in a small building in Washington, DC. The DEA's lobby included an entrance to a seedy bar, the Blue Mirror, which Feldkamp describes as "a big-time watering hole" for many DEA agents. Does Feldkamp remember that the DEA's first precursor agency was dedicated to eliminating alcohol from America?

Similar ironies abound. I talked to a 22-year-old student at the museum. I'd overheard him murmuring appreciatively about the many cannabis pipes on display. It was clear he had smoked and enjoyed pot, so it surprised me when he said he'd just completed an internship with Interpol, and was considering a job with the DEA.

"I don't believe in [the drug war]," he admitted, "but it's an exciting job with good benefits. Gotta go where the money is."

I tried to question [director of the DEA museum Sean] Fearns about his museum's inaccurate, one-sided history of drugs, and about the ironies and tragedies created by the drug war. He refused to even consider my questions.

"Frankly, I'm not here to get into a discussion of politics," he said.

Later, I realized he was scared of marijuana and people who use it.

"The pro-drug organization NORML [National Organization for the Reform of Marijuana Laws] was having a conference in Maryland in 1999, and they wanted to check out the museum," Fearns recalled. "Our security people made me nervous by throwing a lot of worst-case scenarios at us, like what if they came in and did some kind of civil disobedience like the animal rights activists do, throwing blood on the carpet or spray painting the walls. Our head of security used to work the White House, and is familiar with all kinds of nut cases. But about 18 of them came in, and they looked just like average citizens. They looked like regular Americans. Their only negative comment was: "This is a beautiful building and an expensive operation. What a waste of money."

Periodical Bibliography

The following articles have been selected to supplement the diverse views presented in this chapter.

American Anti-Prohibition League	"Drug Courts—Filling 'Treatment Gap' or Treatment Trap," May 21, 2001. www.christiansforcannabis.com.
Chris Brown	"Effective Marijuana Suppression," *Oregon Police Chief Magazine*, Spring 1998.
Richard Cowan	"Conference on Rehab Racketeers Tied to Bush Will Raise Important Issues: Saving Children from Drug Treatment Abuse. Saving DEAland from Drug War Lite. A Conference That Should Embarrass Washington," *Marijuana News*, May 18, 2001.
Family Council on Drug Awareness	"DARE: Good Intentions, Bad Results." www.fcda.org.
Florida Department of Law Enforcement	"Domestic Marijuana Eradication Program 2002 Annual Report," February 2003. www.fdle.state.fl.us.
Jake Ginsky	"Drug Mistreatment," *Mother Jones*, February 18, 2000.
Asa Hutchinson	Speech at the Modernizing Criminal Justice Conference, June 18, 2002. www.drugwar.com.
Jennifer Mertens	"DARE Prevailing in Prevention and Protection," *Law Enforcement Technology*, November 2003.
Ethan A. Nadelmann	"No Longer Hope for Progress," *Counselor: The Magazine for Addiction Professionals*, August 2002.
National Organization for the Reform of Marijuana Laws	"Feds' Pot Eradication Program Seizes Nothing but Ditchweed Hemp, Not Marijuana Focus of DEA Effort, Report Shows," October 4, 2001. www.norml.org.
National Youth Anti-Drug Media Campaign	"Marijuana Prevention Initiative," Office of National Drug Control Policy, April 7, 2003. www.mediacampaign.org.
Margot Roosevelt	"Busted!" *Time*, August 4, 2003.
Ken Sullivan	"Lessons Learned from Public Service Announcements Throughout the Ages," *Koala Online*. www.thekoala.org.
Hal Turner	"Drug War May Soon Become Much Deadlier," *Hal Turner Show*, October 6, 2001.

For Further Discussion

Chapter 1

1. Joseph M. Rey, Andres Martin, and Peter Krabman contend that marijuana is harmful and addictive. Lester Grinspoon, James B. Bakalar, and Ethan Russo make the opposite claim. After examining the six authors' credentials, which trio do you consider more credible, and why?

2. The Office of National Drug Control Policy and its director, John P. Walters, assert that the potency of marijuana is up to thirty times higher today than it was in the 1970s. Daniel Forbes, however, believes that the comparison is faulty because it compares the worst-quality marijuana of the past and the best-quality marijuana known today. With which argument do you agree? Explain why.

3. NORML's mission is to reform state and federal marijuana laws and to ultimately legalize the drug. Does knowing the organization's goals affect your evaluation of its argument that marijuana causes only a slight impairment and does not appear to be responsible for most traffic accidents? Why or why not?

Chapter 2

1. Iain Murray uses statistics by the Justice Department to support his view that few people are incarcerated for simple possession of marijuana or for first-time offenses. Pete Brady uses a different set of statistics and specific examples to show that drug laws target minor marijuana offenders. Which author uses evidence more convincingly? Explain your answer.

2. Medical marijuana user Christopher Largen asserts that laws that prohibit possession of marijuana prevent suffering patients from using an effective medicine. Researcher Eric A. Voth believes that the laws protect patients from a drug that has not been found to be safe or effective. Which argument is more persuasive, in your opinion? Explain.

3. Sherry F. Colb accuses the Justice Department of making an example of Ed Rosenthal, who is one of many medical marijuana growers and distributors across the country. Laura M. Nagel, on the other hand, asserts that prosecuting people who violate federal laws governing drug use is necessary in order to shield people from dangerous drugs. In what ways do you think that federally prosecuting medical marijuana growers protects the

public? In what ways does it harm society? Explain your answer using facts from the viewpoints.

Chapter 3

1. Ethan Nadelmann compares the laws against marijuana use and possession to alcohol prohibition in the 1920s, claiming that both have failed because people use substances even if they are illegal. In contrast, John P. Walters contends that when a drug is legal, use of it increases. To support his view, he claims that alcohol use is higher than marijuana use. Do you think marijuana prohibition reduces marijuana usage? Explain why, supporting your answer with quotes from the viewpoints.

2. The Office of National Drug Control Policy and John P. Walters argue that legalizing marijuana would not stop drug dealers from selling it illegally. R. Keith Stroup posits that the underground market would be eliminated if the drug were legalized. With which opinion do you agree, and why?

Chapter 4

1. Brett and Leann Richardson maintain that D.A.R.E. does not encourage kids to report their parents' marijuana use to police. Dan Savage makes the opposite claim. With whose assertion do you agree? Develop your answer using evidence from the viewpoints.

2. NIDA states that high-sensation anti-marijuana messages attract teens' attention and thus deter drug use. Rich Lowry, in contrast, believes that these ads are dismissed by youth because they are too sensationalized. Which view do you support, and why?

3. Susan Sampl, Ronald Kadden, and Richard Cowan claim that adolescent marijuana users are often referred to treatment by the justice system. Do you think treatment should be mandated for marijuana users who do not wish to quit? Citing the viewpoints, explain why you think mandatory treatment would or would not be effective.

4. Karen Tandy maintains that the Drug Enforcement Administration's marijuana suppression program is necessary to reduce marijuana use and has been effective thus far. Pete Brady concedes that the DEA has successfully destroyed marijuana crops but asserts that its actions harm people and the environment in the process. In your opinion, has the marijuana suppression plan been effective? Why or why not?

Organizations to Contact

Americans for Safe Access (ASA)
1700 Shattuck Ave., #317, Berkeley, CA 94709
(888) 929-4367 • fax: (510) 486-8090
e-mail: info@safeaccessnow.org
Web site: www.safeaccessnow.org

ASA is a national grassroots coalition working with local, state, and national legislators to protect the rights of patients and doctors to legally use marijuana for medical purposes. It provides legal training for lawyers and patients, medical information for doctors and patients, media support for court cases, activist training for grassroots organizers, and rapid response to law enforcement encounters. ASA sends out *Weekly News Summaries* to update its members on legal cases and current events pertaining to marijuana.

Common Sense for Drug Policy
1377-C Spencer Ave., Lancaster, PA 17603
(717) 299-0600 • fax: (717) 393-4953
e-mail: info@csdp.org • Web site: www.csdp.org

Common Sense for Drug Policy is a nonprofit organization dedicated to expanding the discussion on drug policy by voicing questions about existing laws and educating the public about alternatives to current policies. It offers advice and technical assistance to individuals and organizations working to reform current policies, hosts public forums, and provides pro bono legal assistance to those adversely affected by drug policy. It makes available numerous news articles, links, and fact sheets, including "Drug War Facts," on its Web site.

Drug Enforcement Administration (DEA)
Mailstop AXS, 2401 Jefferson Davis Hwy., Alexandria, VA 22301
(202) 307-1000
Web site: www.dea.gov

The DEA is the federal agency charged with enforcing the nation's drug laws. The organization concentrates on stopping the smuggling and distribution of narcotics in the United States and abroad. It publishes *Microgram Journal* biannually, *Microgram Bulletins* monthly, and drug prevention booklets, such as *Get It Straight* and *Speaking Out Against Drug Legalization*.

Drug Policy Alliance
70 W. Thirty-sixth St., Sixteenth Fl., New York, NY 10018
(212) 613-8020 • fax: (212) 613-8021
e-mail: nyc@drugpolicy.org
Web site: www.drugpolicyalliance.com

The alliance, an independent nonprofit organization, supports and publicizes alternatives to current U.S. policies on illegal drugs, including marijuana. To keep Americans informed, the Drug Policy Alliance compiles newspaper articles on drug legalization issues and distributes legislative updates. Its publications include the *Ally* newsletter and the book *It's Just a Plant*.

Family Research Council
801 G St. NW, Washington, DC 20001
(202) 393-2100 • (800) 225-4008 • fax: (202) 393-2134
e-mail: corrdept@frc.org • Web site: www.frc.org

The council analyzes issues affecting the family and seeks to ensure that the interests of the traditional family are considered in the formulation of public policy. It lobbies legislatures and promotes public debate on issues concerning the family. The council publishes articles and position papers against the legalization of medicinal marijuana.

Marijuana Policy Project
PO Box 77492, Capitol Hill, Washington, DC 20013
(202) 462-5747 • fax: (202) 232-0442
e-mail: mpp@mpp.org • Web site: www.mpp.org

The Marijuana Policy Project develops and promotes policies to minimize the harm associated with marijuana laws. The project increases public awareness through speaking engagements, educational seminars, and the mass media. Briefing papers and news articles as well as the quarterly *MPP Report* can be accessed on its Web site.

National Center on Addiction and Substance Abuse (CASA)
633 Third Ave., 19th Fl., New York, NY 10017-6706
(212) 841-5200
Web site: www.casacolumbia.org

CASA is a private nonprofit organization that works to educate the public about the hazards of chemical dependency. The organization supports treatment as the best way to reduce chemical dependency. It produces numerous publications describing the harmful effects of alcohol and drug addiction and effective ways to address the problem of substance abuse.

National Institute on Drug Abuse (NIDA)
National Institutes of Health
6001 Executive Blvd., Room 5213, Bethesda, MD 20892
(301) 443-1124
e-mail: information@lists.nida.nih.gov
Web site: www.nida.nih.gov

NIDA supports and conducts research on drug abuse to improve addiction prevention, treatment, and policy efforts. It is dedicated to understanding how abused drugs affect the brain and behavior, and it works to rapidly disseminate new information to policy makers, drug abuse treatment practitioners, other health care practitioners and the general public. It prints the bimonthly *NIDA Notes* newsletter, *NIDA Capsules* fact sheets, and a catalog of research reports and public education materials, such as *Marijuana: Facts for Teens* and *Mind over Matter.*

National Organization for the Reform of Marijuana Laws (NORML)
1600 K St. NW, Suite 501, Washington, DC 20006-2832
(202) 483-5500 • fax: (202) 483-0057
e-mail: norml@norml.org • Web site: www.norml.org

NORML fights to legalize marijuana and to help those who have been convicted or sentenced for possessing or selling marijuana. It asserts that marijuana can, and should, be used responsibly by adults who so choose. In addition to pamphlets and position papers, NORML publishes weekly press releases, a weekly E-zine, and the *Leaflet* and *Legislative Bulletin* newsletters.

Office of National Drug Control Policy (ONDCP)
Drug Policy Information Clearinghouse
PO Box 6000, Rockville, MD 20849-6000
(800) 666-3332 • fax: (301) 519-5212
e-mail: ondcp@ncjrs.org
Web site: www.whitehousedrugpolicy.gov

The Office of National Drug Control Policy is responsible for formulating the government's national drug strategy and the president's antidrug policy as well as coordinating the federal agencies responsible for stopping drug trafficking. It has launched drug prevention programs, including the National Youth Anti-Drug Media Campaign, which focuses on the dangers of marijuana. ONDCP publications include *Marijuana Myths & Facts: The Truth Behind Ten Popular Misperceptions, What Americans Need to Know About Marijuana,* and "Marijuana Fact Sheet."

RAND Drug Policy Research Center

PO Box 2138, Santa Monica, CA 90407-2138
(310) 393-0411 • fax: (310) 393-4818
e-mail: dprc@rand.org • Web site: www.rand.org

The RAND Corporation is a research institution that seeks to improve public policy through research and analysis. RAND's Drug Policy Research Center disseminates information on the costs, prevention, and treatment of alcohol and drug abuse as well as on trends in drug-law enforcement. Its extensive list of publications includes the research brief *How State Medical Marijuana Laws Vary: A Comprehensive Review* and the book *An Ounce of Prevention, a Pound of Uncertainty: The Cost-Effectiveness of School-Based Drug Prevention Programs.*

Bibliography of Books

Joan Bello — *The Benefits of Marijuana: Physical, Psychological, and Spiritual.* Boca Raton, FL: Lifeservices Press, 2001.

Alan Bock — *Waiting to Inhale: The Politics of Medical Marijuana.* Santa Ana, CA: Seven Locks Press, 2000.

Mitch Earleywine — *Understanding Marijuana: A New Look at Scientific Evidence.* Oxford, UK: Oxford University Press, 2002.

M.A. ElSohly and S.A. Ross — *Quarterly Report: Potency Monitoring Project.* Oxford: University of Mississippi, November 2004.

Jon Gettman and the NORML Foundation — *United States Marijuana Arrests.* Part Two. *Racial Differences in Drug Arrests.* Washington, DC: National Organization for the Reform of Marijuana Laws, 2000.

Mike Gray — *Busted: Stone Cowboys, Narco-Lords, and Washington's War on Drugs.* New York: Thunder's Mouth Press/Nation Books, 2002.

Lester Grinspoon and James B. Bakalar — *Marijuana, the Forbidden Medicine.* New Haven, CT: Yale University Press, 1997.

Jalil Guillermo — *Street-Wise Drug Prevention: A Realistic Approach to Prevent and Intervene in Adolescent Drug Use.* Reading, PA: No More Drugs, 1996.

ImpacTeen Illicit Drug Team — *Illicit Drug Policies: Selected Laws from the Fifty States.* Berrien Springs, MI: Andrews University, 2002.

Leslie L. Iversen — *The Science of Marijuana.* New York: Oxford University Press, 2000.

Janet E. Joy, Stanley J. Watson Jr., and John A. Benson Jr., eds. — *Marijuana and Medicine: Assessing the Science Base.* Washington, DC: National Academy Press, 1999.

Robert J. MacCoun and Peter Reuter — *Drug War Heresies: Learning from Other Vices, Times, and Places.* Cambridge, MA: Cambridge University Press, 2001.

Marijuana Anonymous — *Life with Hope: A Return to Living Through the Twelve Steps and Twelve Traditions of Marijuana Anonymous.* Van Nuys, CA: A New Leaf, 1995.

George McMahon and Christopher Largen — *Prescription Pot: A Leading Advocate's Heroic Battle to Legalize Medical Marijuana.* Far Hills, NJ: New Horizon Press, 2003.

National Center on
Addiction and
Substance Abuse at
Columbia University

*Non-Medical Marijuana II: Rite of Passage or
Russian Roulette.* New York: Columbia University, April 2004.

Office of National
Drug Control Policy

*The Challenge in Higher Education: Confronting
and Reducing Substance Abuse on Campus.* Washington, DC: Office of National Drug Control
Policy, 2004.

Office of National
Drug Control Policy

National Drug Control Strategy Update, 2003.
Washington, DC: Office of National Drug
Control Policy, 2003.

Rosalie Liccardo
Pacula, Jamie F.
Chriqui, and
Joanna King

*Marijuana Decriminalization: What Does It Mean
in the United States?* Santa Monica, CA: Rand,
2004.

RoperASW

*Partnership Attitude Tracking Study, 2003: Teens
Study: Survey of Teens' Attitudes and Behaviors
Toward Marijuana.* New York: Partnership for a
Drug-Free America, 2003.

Ed Rosenthal and
William Logan

Ask Ed's Marijuana Law: Don't Get Busted.
Oakland, CA: Quick American, 2000.

Sue Rusche

*A Guide to the Drug Legalization Movement and
How YOU Can Stop It!* Atlanta: National Families in Action, 1997.

Eric Schlosser

*Reefer Madness: Sex, Drugs, and Cheap Labor in
the American Black Market.* Boston: Houghton
Mifflin, 2003.

Substance Abuse and
Mental Health
Services Administration

Tips for Teens: The Truth About Marijuana.
Rockville, MD: Center for Substance Abuse
Prevention, 2000.

Jacob Sullum

Saying Yes: In Defense of Drug Use. Los Angeles:
Tarcher/Putnam, May 2003.

Westat and Annenberg
School for
Communication at
the University of
Pennsylvania

*Evaluation of the National Youth Anti-Drug Media
Campaign: 2003 Report of Findings.* Rockville,
MD: Westat, December 22, 2003.

Lynn Zimmer
and John Morgan

*Marijuana Myths, Marijuana Facts: A Review of
the Scientific Evidence.* New York: Lindesmith
Center, 1997.